# THAT THEY MIGHT BE ONE

*From the Father's Embrace*

*to the Miracle of a Unified Heart*

KARI ANN RIVADENEIRA

© 2026 by Kari Ann Rivadeneira

No part of this publication may be reproduced, distributed, or transmitted in any form or by any means, including photocopying, recording, or other electronic or mechanical methods, without the prior written permission of the publisher, except in the case of brief quotations embodied in critical reviews and certain other noncommercial uses permitted by copyright law.

**Aletheia Publishing**

ISBN: 979-8-9946202-0-5

Printed in the United States of America First Edition, 2026

Scripture Acknowledgments Unless otherwise indicated, all Scripture quotations are taken from the New King James Version® (NKJV).
Copyright © 1982 by Thomas Nelson. Used by permission. All rights reserved.

# DEDICATION

---

**To Ramiro, Abigale, and Makayla.**

May the truths in these pages be the soil of our own family's Eden. As we walk together, may we always choose love—the bond of perfection— and live out our days in the seamless oneness of His Spirit.

# Table of Contents

# FOREWARD

There are books that inform us, books that inspire us, and books that rearrange us.

*That They Might Be One* belongs unapologetically to the third category.

From the first page, you can feel it: this is not a book written to impress the mind or to win an argument. It is written from a place of encounter. Of wrestling. Of surrender. Of long obedience in the same direction. This book was not born out of theory—it was born out of communion.

Jesus' prayer in John 17 is not poetic sentiment. It is not aspirational language. It is a priestly prayer spoken on the edge of the cross, offered with blood already in view. *"That they may be one, as We are one."* Not agreement. Not uniformity. Not performance. Union.

And that is exactly where Kari writes from.

What makes this book so disarming—and so necessary—is that it refuses to let unity remain an abstract theological idea. Instead, it takes unity out of the clouds and places it squarely in the places we often try to avoid: marriages, friendships, conflict, parenting, spiritual warfare, shame, correction, intimacy, and the slow, holy work of love being formed in real people.

This is not a call to "try harder" or "do better." It is an invitation to *abide deeper*.

Kari writes with the rare combination of clarity and tenderness that only comes from someone who has allowed the Holy Spirit to search the heart—not once, but continually. She does not speak *at* the reader. She walks *with* them. She names what many of us feel but haven't had language for: the exhaustion of striving, the confusion between gifting and fruit, the quiet ache for connection that rules cannot heal.

At the center of this book is a truth the Church desperately needs to remember:

*Unity does not begin with behavior—it begins with belonging.*

True oneness is not forged through control, fear, or sameness. It is formed when people come alive to their belovedness, when shame loses its voice, when love becomes the operating system instead of a side effect. Kari does not shy away from confronting broken paradigms—but she does it the way Jesus does: with light, not accusation.

Perhaps the most profound gift of this book is how relentlessly it re-centers everything on love—not sentimental love but transforming love. The kind of love that dismantles fear. The kind that ends the need for enemies. The kind that exposes the lie that people are the problem when the real battle has already been won.

As you read these pages, you may find yourself slowed down. You may feel exposed—not in a condemning way, but in a *safe* way. You may recognize areas where you have confused activity with intimacy, or unity with compliance. If that happens, don't rush past it. That pause is holy. That is the Spirit doing what He does best: leading us back into truth through kindness.

This book is not trying to build a system.

It is calling us back to a family.

It reminds us that the prayer Jesus prayed is not fragile. It will be answered. And the way it will be answered is not through force—but through love made complete in willing hearts.

I believe *That They Might Be One* has arrived at exactly the right time.

Not because the Church needs another message—but because it needs a reminder of who it already is.

Read slowly. Read prayerfully.

And let yourself be undone and re-woven by the same love that has been holding you all along.

Carrie Hattaway

*Kingdom Life Women*

# PREFACE

The night before the crucifixion, Jesus knelt and prayed the last words that His lips would utter this side of heaven. He knew the heavy, military like footsteps of the Roman guard, led by the Pharisees and religious leaders would very soon be heard coming into the Garden of Gethsemane. He knew He would experience the betrayal of all His followers, the rejection of His own people, and utter humiliation and tortuous physical pain in the next few hours.

He could have prayed many things, but Jesus specifically chose *certain* things in His requests to the Father. First, He prayed for Himself that He would glorify the Father. Next,

He prayed for His disciples. He prayed that the Father would keep them from evil, and that they would be sanctified by truth.

Finally, Jesus prayed for all believers. The very first thing He prayed was, "that they all *may be one,* as You, Father, are in Me, and I in You..." (John 17:1-21). Of all the things that Jesus could pray, *He prayed for oneness.*

What He prayed must have shaken the principalities. *Oneness?*

This is no small miracle. If you're married, or have had close friends and family, you know even inside the most intimate of relationships, there are disagreements. At times, these can be chaotic disruptions that hardly resemble oneness. If two people have a hard time getting along all the time, how in the world can Jesus pray that *all believers* would have the oneness that He shared with the Father and the Spirit?

*Jesus prayed for oneness* when the religious leaders of His own people, the Pharisees and Sadducees, who constantly disagreed on doctrine attacked Him. *Oneness* when the Church leaders of the day openly persecuted, mocked, and tried to trap Jesus. *Oneness* when the Roman officials and the Jews came together in agreement to murder an innocent man. *Oneness* when many of His followers thought the Kingdom of God was coming as a military Kingdom, and perhaps not one single person understood Jesus' mission. *Oneness* amid His own disciples leaving Him completely alone in His hour of betrayal.

I have heard of certain denominations claiming that their church is the fulfillment of this "oneness" prayer from Jesus because they all have the same sermons, and all read the same scripture every day. Although I value reading and learning the same thing with others, this is a far cry short of what Jesus had in mind. One denomination doesn't have the answer- and the proof is that *there are denominations.* Denominations are formed because of division. That's *not* the oneness that Jesus was describing.

With man, this is impossible, but with God, all things are possible. (Matt. 19:26). This book explores the journey into that oneness—a reality that begins not in our effort to get along, but in our individual union with the Father's heart. It will only come to pass by His people uniting with His heart and seeing oneness come to all hearts.

For a group of people to be one, they must have a single heart. That single personal heart will then be healthy enough to have strong relationships with others. Oneness begins with each person experiencing oneness with God. From that place of acceptance, love and affirmation, they can then begin to experience oneness with one another. It all begins in God and ends in God. This isn't about agreeing on every point of doctrine; it's about sharing the same pulse.

We must realize that *proximity is not union*; we can stand side-by-side and still be worlds apart until we experience oneness with God.

One thing I can count on:  Jesus will get His prayers answered. *We will be one.*

# That They Might Be One

# CHAPTER ONE

## Did You Learn to Love?

My husband and I watch a show on the History Channel called, "Alone." They take men or women and place them in an undeveloped, cold, and harsh climates. The contestants are placed there completely... well, *alone.* They must make their own shelter and procure their own food. They must do this without the help of anyone. There is no camera crew, no spouses, no children and no friends. It's an outdoor solitary confinement.

Many contestants quit in the first few weeks simply because they miss their family. As the show progresses, and the days turn into weeks that turn into months, even people who profess to enjoy living solidary lives begin to break. They will cry, film themselves discussing their parents or family at length, and begin to have depressing thoughts.

Most of them begin to talk about how they are having an incredible experience; but having no one else there to share the experience robs them of the joy that experience could contain. Many times, we have seen the contestants break down sobbing, wishing they could share the joy of catching a fish with *anyone*.

On the 2024 season of Alone, there were two men left at the end. Both had enough food, and warm shelter to continue to brave the harsh winter conditions. One of the men, Timber Cleghorn, suddenly and abruptly decided to leave the competition. Although there was half a million dollars on the table, he simply could not stand another day being away from his wife and children. The pull of family and connection was so strong, not even money could keep him away. Not even money that could change his family's life!

Humans were designed for intimate, close connection with others. Without that connection, part of them start to die.

That's why God said, "it is not good that man is alone..." (Genesis 2:18).

At the core of every close, meaningful relationship that humans have, intimacy exists. Intimacy is required for close, personal connection. Not only is it central to human relationships, but also the core of our relationship with God.

The word intimacy can immediately cause a reaction in people. Some smile, thinking of beautiful times with their spouse or loved one, but some feel shameful, pull back in fear, or feel disgusted. Some have no paradigm whatsoever for what intimacy means. This is a massive problem, because intimacy is the core of our relationship with our Father, Abba, the Son Jesus and Holy Spirit. If we do not know what intimacy is, how can we begin to know God?

---

*Without intimacy, there is no love.*

---

Without intimacy, there is no love. Without love, there is no relationship. For a relationship to thrive and be healthy, it must be rooted in love and nurtured by intimacy.

In the pages that follow, we are going to strip away the shame and the performance and look at intimacy for what it truly is: the fuel for everything you were created to be.

The early church was a thriving community of people, going house to house, and breaking bread with one another. They were not chatting on cell phones or having long distance relationship. These people lived life together. They experienced the blessing and prosperity that close, meaningful relationships produce. I'm afraid over time, we have become people that don't know their neighbors and hide behind walls of "mind your own business." Because of this, I believe the church suffers. When walls are up, people do not have access to the help that their friendship groups could readily provide.

No man is an island. We were created to experience life together.

When Jesus was on the Earth, He made a very interesting statement. He said that He would send the Holy Spirit to humanity when He had gone to the Father. John 16:7 says, "Nevertheless I tell you the truth. It is to your advantage that I go away; *for if I do not go away*, the Helper will not come to you; but if I depart, I will send Him to you."

Why did Jesus have to depart and go back to the Father before the Holy Spirit was sent? Perhaps it is because God is love, and love is only love when it is shared with someone else. One person cannot love, because love must flow somewhere. The essence of love is to share with another. Jesus could not leave the Father alone, and He was not going to leave Holy Spirit alone. Before the Holy Spirit was sent to the Earth to remain, He was with the Father. Jesus had us here on the Earth.

Love always must have someone else to flow through, or it ceases to be love. If love itself requires more than one, then most of what we must learn in this age is how to interact with other humans.

Bob Jones was a prophet who died on Valentine's Day in 2014. Before he died, he had a profound near-death experience in August 1975. During this experience, he found himself standing before the Lord in heaven. As he was waiting to enter, he heard the Lord asking each person ahead of him, "Did you learn to love?"

Bob was prepared to answer "yes" and enter heaven, but the Lord stopped him. He asked Bob to return to earth with a message for the church: "Did you learn to love?" This near-death experience deeply impacted Bob, and he spoke about it many times after he recovered. There was only one word that God emphasized to him: *love.*

---

*Love always must have someone else to flow through, or it ceases to be love.*

---

## The Fruit and the Gifts

What is the entire goal of our Christian experience? To know love and become love. In fact, Timothy tells us in 1 Timothy 1:5: *"Now the purpose of the commandment* ***is love*** *from a* *pure heart, from a good conscience, and from sincere faith."*

The *entire goal* of scripture is so that we would love. All the historical stories, the proverbs, the healings, teachings and parables pointed to this: *Love is the chief goal.* Without love, we are nothing.

The Apostle Paul wrote a very famous chapter on love: 1 Corinthians 13. In his letter to the Corinthian church, Paul starts off by writing, "If I have the gift of prophecy and can fathom all mysteries and all knowledge, and if I have a faith that can move mountains, but do not have love, I am nothing" (1 Corinthians 13:2). Did you notice that he started off by talking about the *gifts* of the Holy Spirit, not the *fruit* of the Holy Spirit? You could have the *gift*, but *be nothing*, according to Paul.

Paul said that you can have all the gifting in the world, but if there is *no love*, it's worthless.

There is a big difference between the gifts of the Holy Spirit and the fruit of the Holy Spirit. What the apostle Paul is trying to encourage the church with is this: it doesn't do any good to have a "gift" without "fruit."

Gifts are from God. The gifts God gives us are wisdom, knowledge, faith, healing, miraculous powers, prophecy, distinguishing between spirits, speaking in different kinds of tongues, and interpretation of tongues (1 Cor. 12:8-10,28-30). There are also gifts of prophecy, serving, teaching, encouragement, giving, leading, and showing mercy

(Romans 12:6-8). Lastly, Ephesians 4:11-12 tell us the major “office” gifts: apostles, prophets, evangelists, pastors and teachers.

These gifts will flow out of people whether they have an intimate prayer life with God or not. There are many unbelievers who are excellent teachers. There are unsaved men and women who are the most generous people, and many people serve who don’t know God at all. Even believers, if they are far away from the Lord but at one time confessed Him as Lord, will operate in the giftings that God gave them.

A gift only has one qualification: that you receive it. God isn’t a “take-backs” giver. Once He gives it, it’s yours for the keeping, whether you stay in intimate fellowship with Him or wander away. He gives and will allow you to walk away from Him if you choose *with* your gift in hand.

Romans 11:29 says, “For the gifts and the calling of God are without repentance.” Another way of saying that verse is that the gifts God gives are not dependent upon us having a repentant heart or changing the way we think. The word for repentance is “metanoia” in Greek, and it means "a radical mind shift.” The word is broken down into two components: meta (meaning "together with" or "with") and nous (meaning "mind"). The word means you must change how you *think*, rather than the traditional translation of "repentance," which often carries connotations of changing your *behavior*.

The only way we can change the way we think is by renewing our minds with the Word of God. As we meditate on the

Word, God empowers us to think the way He thinks. We are transformed into His same image when we do this. (2 Cor. 3:18).

What does it mean, then, that the gifts of God are *without changing the way you think*? The gifts of God will work in you whether you "metanoia" or not. You don't have to change the way you think to have a gift. That means you can see signs, miracles, tongues, generosity, prophecy or wisdom in someone who has a completely *unrepentant* heart and mind.

Just because God does a miracle through someone is not a stamp of approval from God on their life.

On the other hand, the *fruit* of the Spirit is only evident in a life that has been abiding in God. These are *only* evident when a person is intimate in prayer with God. When Paul listed all the gifts in 1 Corinthians 13, he ended his conclusion of love with this statement: "And now these three remain: *faith*, *hope* and *love*. But the greatest of these is **love**."

---

*The fruit of the Spirit is only evident in a life that has been abiding in God.*

---

Love is the primary motivator for any of the gifts, but you can flow in the gifts without love. We know it's possible, because Paul said it was. He said, “If you have the gift of prophecy... but have not love, I am nothing.”

*You are nothing without love because God is love.* Once the Holy Spirit has come and made His forever home in you, you’ve now permanently accessed the ability to love through His empowerment. This access to the empowerment is directly related to how you steward God’s abiding presence within you.

I believe this is why Jesus spoke about this reality right before He headed to the cross. In John 15, Jesus spoke about what it looks like to stay connected to God, who is our power source. He used a gardening metaphor to teach His disciples about producing fruit:

*“Abide in me, as I also abide in you. No branch can bear fruit by itself; it must abide in the vine. Neither can you bear fruit unless you remain in me. I am the vine; you are the branches. If you remain in me and I in you, you will bear much fruit; apart from me you can do nothing.” (John 15:4-5).*

The fruit of the spirit *cannot* grow in a life outside of abiding in prayer with God. If, however, we remain in life-union with God, we will bear *much* fruit.

Galatians 5:22-23 says, "But the fruit of the Spirit is love, joy, peace, longsuffering, kindness, goodness, faithfulness, gentleness, self-control. Against such there is no law."

Notice the word "fruit" here. In the Greek, it's *karpos*, and it's singular — not "fruits." Paul doesn't list nine separate fruits; he lists one fruit with nine expressions. Love comes first, and everything after it reads like an outworking of love, not nine independent goals to chase. Joy is what love feels like. Peace is what love produces. Patience is what love does when it's tested. In other words, love is the source. All the fruit of the Spirit springs forth from love.

In other words, love is the source. All the fruit of the Spirit spring forth from love.

Many people think that if they move in their gifts, they will be loved and accepted by God. They also believe that if they operate in gifts, they will be loved and accepted more by people. *The opposite is true.* As you enjoy being loved by God, the gifts effortlessly flow out of you fueled by love, producing unity. If you're "earning it," you'll see others as competition. If you're flowing in love, you'll encourage others in the same loving acceptance you've received.

It is fruitful when a dad can speak softly and kindly to his daughter when she's done something wrong. It is evidence of abiding if you can be behind someone slow in traffic and not get bent out of shape. The evidence of Holy Spirit's work in a person when they can stand before their betrayer and keep no record of wrong.

The fruit of the Spirit is necessary to maintain positive, healthy relationships within our marriages, families, and friend circles. Farther than that, fruit directly impacts our cities and communities. To have healthy functioning relationships, the fruit of the Spirit must be evident in our lives.

In the garden of Eden, God first commanded Adam and Eve to be *fruitful and multiply* (Gen. 1:28.) Being fruitful is something that God commanded us to do in our original design; that means that it's possible for us to do this. What God calls us to; He equips us for. I have known many people over the years who say, "This is just how I am. I'm angry, and it's my personality." Anger is not a personality; it's a symptom of the old man apart from the life of Christ. Many others have said, "I'm just not a patient person." The truth is, *you're not patient because you're unloving. And you're unloving because you do not have a full revelation of how much you are loved by God.*

---

*You're not patient because you're unloving. And you're unloving because you do not have a full revelation of how much you are loved by God.*

---

We are unable to be patient with spouses or children *when we don't have a revelation of God's patience towards us.* We are only able to give fruit that we have first received and then sown!

So, how does fruit begin to be formed? First, you must hear the gospel. Colossians 1:5 says, "Because of the hope which is laid up for you in heaven, of which *you heard* before in the word of the truth of the gospel, which has come to you, as it has also in all the world, and is bringing forth fruit, as it is also among you since the day you heard and knew the grace of God in truth."

1. Fruit begins its formation when we hear the word of truth. In other words, the moment we hear the gospel, and receive truth, fruit will be brought forth. *We must first hear the word of truth.*

2. Secondly, all fruit comes from the Spirit. Colossians 1:8 says, "...love *in* the Spirit." 1 Cor 13 lists the fruit of the Spirit, beginning with love. Ephesians 5:9 lists where this fruit is located: it is found *in* goodness, righteousness and truth.

3. Finally, Hebrews 12:11 tells us that God has a way of producing more fruit in us: His loving discipline. "Now no chastening seems to be joyful for the present, but painful; nevertheless, afterward it yields the peaceable fruit of righteousness to those who have been trained by it."

We are more fruitful when we experience the correction of God as a Father. It never seems fun in the moment, but after the correction process has passed, we are able to taste and see the Lord's goodness by experiencing His fruit in our lives.

God's correction always is gentle and kind. Romans 2:4 says that it is the *kindness* of God that leads us to repentance!

When there is an opportunity to correct our children, do we unquestionably, uncompromisingly, use the same gentleness and kindness that God uses with us? For many years in my life, I justified speaking to my children harshly, because it was "my right" as a parent.

However, one day everything changed. I was at home with my two girls- Abby and Makayla. Makayla was having a particularly rough day. A bright, active three-year-old was extra mischievous. After the fourth time I asked her to stop her behavior, and she ignored me, I grabbed her by the arm and carried her into my room. She dangled there, thinking it was a game, and started laughing. That infuriated me, and I flung her to the ground. Now, it was maybe two inches that she fell, but she fell, nonetheless.

Immediately, The Holy Spirit's voice broke through my anger. He said, "*Don't you ever touch my daughter like that again.*" The voice was strong, firm, but deeply gentle. The moment I heard it; I collapsed on the floor next to my daughter and hugged her and apologized over and repeatedly. That day, something deep happened inside me. I realized that anger will *never* bring a child to repentance, and that the Lord had a better way.

More than that, the fear of the Lord came over my heart that Makayla wasn't just my daughter- but she was also *His daughter*, and I was going to be held accountable for my parenting. *He sees it all.* Parental anger is never appropriate when disciplining your children. There is never any hope of good fruit being produced from rotten fruit. I am so grateful that the Lord came and brought *correction to my heart* when I needed it the most. I thought Makayla was the problem, *but it was me.*

I've had people argue this point with me. They say, "Yes, but you don't understand my children. They won't respond to kindness. You have to yell to get your point across. And if they don't listen the first time, they need spankings, and I must raise my voice louder so they can hear, because obviously speaking kindly didn't work."

I can see what they mean. I get you, because I've experienced it and I've done it! However, God has been a parent for a long time, and He's had millions of children. I believe His standard of discipline is the correct one to follow, and scripture is clear: it is the *kindness of God* that leads to repentance. If you want your children, spouse, or friend to change the way they're thinking, *the only scriptural way is through kindness.*

Discipline is very different from punishment, and I began to understand the difference after my God encounter with Makayla. God never punishes us to make us more fruitful. Rather, He gives us boundaries to grow. If we grow outside those boundaries, His discipline will lovingly, gently, bring correction if we are His sons and daughters.

When I experienced God’s correction over my treatment of my daughter, I was then able to begin to understand how to bring correction to my children. I’m still learning!

The journey of growing in the Spirit and bearing fruit is a continuous process of learning, correction, and embracing God's loving discipline. When we understand and then apply God’s kindness and gentleness, we can foster a nurturing environment for ourselves and those around us. Just as God delights in watching His garden grow, we too can find joy in witnessing the transformation and spiritual growth that occurs as we align our hearts with His will, ultimately producing a bountiful harvest of fruit of the Spirit!

# CHAPTER TWO

# Bearing Fruit

Of all the things that God could have made to place man in, He chose a garden, the Garden of Eden. Why a garden? Because, I believe, that God likes watching things grow. God, who can make everything anything He wants it to be, chose the growing process because He likes it. Genesis 8:22 says, "While the earth remains, seed, time and harvest... shall not cease." He designed seed, time, and harvest.

If God likes watching things grow and doesn't expect nor demand a seed to be a fully mature fruit producing machine, then it's worth looking at the biblical process of seed to fruit.

---

*If God doesn't demand a seed to be a fully mature fruit-producing machine, why do we?*

---

Have you ever wondered why God didn't make vegetables of the spirit instead of fruit of the spirit? There is one thing that separates vegetables from fruit: one produces seeds within itself, and the other does not. Every single fruit *has seeds* within itself that will produce more of its kind.

In the beginning, God made everything after its own kind. The word kind means, "a sort, species." Specifically, this means that bananas don't have seeds to grow asparagus, or that dogs can't mate with dolphins, or that trees don't have the ability to reproduce leopards. In His kingdom, God put the same "kind" of seed of reproduction inside everything He created. Let's specifically look, however, at the way that

## Bearing Fruit

God made vegetation grow because we're discussing fruit. "Then God said, 'Let the land produce vegetation: seed-bearing plants and trees on the land that bear fruit with seed in it, according to their various kinds.' And it was so." - Genesis 1:11

God's design in creating plants that reproduce "*according to their kinds*" through <u>seeds.</u>

The seed is "*in*" itself. Whatever will grow will come from a seed that has been sown. In fact, Jesus said, "Most assuredly, I say to you, unless a grain of wheat falls into the ground and dies, it remains alone; but if it dies, it produces much grain" (John 12:24). The purpose of a seed going into the ground is to die. But the death of that one seed will produce a limitless number of more seeds for more trees for more fruit.

A teacher once asked me, "How many trees are in this acorn seed?" The answer- it's limitless. One seeds' death will just simply keep multiplying in reproduction if the conditions are right. 1 Peter 1:23 says that you and I have been born again of *incorruptible* seed. The word incorruptible in the Greek is *aphthartos*, which means un-decaying, or immortal. You were born to live forever.

Now here's the jaw-dropping amazing work that Christ did: when He died, *you* died. Galatians 2:20 says, "I have been crucified with Christ; it is no longer I who live, but Christ lives in me; and the life which I now live in the flesh I live by faith in the Son of God, who loved me and gave Himself for me." When Christ died, *He died as us, and with us*. Because

He was the seed that went into the ground and died, we also died with Him. Because we are incorruptible seed that is immortal, we can now produce a great harvest of fruit!

This reality is so profound, John the Beloved penned, "Whoever has been born of God does not sin, for His seed remains in him; and he cannot sin, because he has been born of God" (1 John 3:9). Can you wrap your mind around God empowering you to such a degree that you *cannot sin?*

The "Incorruptible Seed" (Christ in you) cannot sin, and as we *abide* (seamless union), that nature dominates our behavior.

I have often heard people say things like "I just don't understand how you can pray so long." Or "my personality is different. I just don't like reading scripture." Or "my wife does all the praying for us both because I don't have time." Or "I'm not a very good reader so I let other people read the Word for me. It doesn't make any sense to me."

If we lower the standard of fruit bearing to what we feel like we can fit with in our own personalities, or timeframe, we will never see the fruit that is possible inside of God. Jesus, as a *man,* holds the standard of what a flourishing, fruitful prayer life looks like. He never lost His temper, yelled at His disciples, or behaved rudely, because He *is* perfectly fruitful.

Now that we've established that God likes watching things grow, and that He designed seed, time, and harvest, and that we've been born of incorruptible seed, we need to take a close look into the next step: exactly what does a fruit seed need to grow?

### 1: The Seed

You and I have been created from an incorruptible seed that is enduring and eternal. As Scripture declares, "Having been born again, not of corruptible seed but incorruptible, through the word of God which lives and abides forever" (1 Peter 1:23). This means our spiritual rebirth is rooted in a seed that cannot decay or perish, ensuring that the core of our lives is born of God. What we have received from God is everlasting and unchanging.

### 2: The Sun

The Sun is essential for all life and growth, and the Word tells us that Jesus' face shines like the sun. Revelation 1:16 says, "His countenance was like the sun shining in its strength," and Matthew 17:2 recounts, "He was transfigured before them. His face shone like the sun, and His clothes became as white as the light." Just as the sun provides powerful light and energy for seeds to grow, Jesus' radiant presence brings life and transformation to those who seek Him. As we behold Him in prayer, it's like soaking in the sun. It's not work; its exposure.

### 3: Water

Water is vital for growth, and in the spiritual life, the Holy Spirit serves as this living water, accessible to every believer. Scripture promises that those who believe in Christ will experience rivers of living water flowing from within, empowering them to flourish and thrive (John 7:38). Just as a tree planted by rivers of water bears fruit in its season and its leaves never wither, so too does the life nourished by the Spirit prosper in everything (Psalm 1:3). Wherever the river of God's presence flows, life abounds and transformation occurs, echoing the assurance that everything touched by this river will live (Ezekiel 47:9). The river of the Holy Spirit flows out of you, bringing refreshment everywhere you go!

### 4: Soil Quality

Soil quality is essential for growth, and in our spiritual lives, it means being rooted and grounded in love. As Ephesians 3:17 declares, "That Christ may dwell in your hearts through faith; that you, being rooted and grounded in love..." This foundation of love enables us to grow deeply and securely, just as healthy soil allows a seed to develop strong roots and flourish.

### 5: Temperature/Environment

Temperature and environment are crucial factors for growth, both in the natural and spiritual realms. Spiritually, we are assured that our environment is established in the heavenly places with Christ, as Scripture says, "And raised us up together and made us sit together in the heavenly places in Christ Jesus" (Eph. 2:6). Just as the right temperature and environment are necessary for a seed to flourish, being positioned in the presence of Christ provides the perfect spiritual climate for us to thrive and bear fruit in our lives.

### 6: Pruning and Training/ Support Structures

Just as pruning and training are necessary for a healthy vineyard, so too does God lovingly discipline those He calls His own. Though discipline may feel difficult or even painful in the moment, Scripture assures us that it ultimately yields a harvest of righteousness and peace for those who accept its guidance and allow themselves to be shaped by it (Hebrews 12:11). The Father draws fruitless branches closer to Himself, and, as Jesus taught, "Every branch in Me that does not bear fruit He takes away; and every branch that bears fruit He prunes, that it may bear more fruit" (John 15:2). Through this process, God's care and correction enable us to grow stronger and become even more fruitful in our lives.

When you add all these elements together, you will have a very fruitful vineyard. This is what the experience of prayer *feels* like for me. I feel the sun of His face when I pray. I experience the sensation of water flowing through me, and His love empowering me. Because I have meditated for years on the life of Holy Spirit being a river in me, I experience the sensation. Because I have pondered His love casting out all fear, I sometimes feel a warmth of His presence around me.

I know that the roots of my life are anchored to His love. I have intimately known His embrace when I feel like I have failed the most. These were never meant to be just words on a page, but they were meant to translate into realities that we *experience* and live in!

If you just memorize these as facts, you will never experience the life of the growth of any seeds. Head knowledge will only puff you up, because it's love that does the edifying (1 Cor. 8:1). The spirit of revelation always *hits the heart first*, and then the heart teaches the mind and brings you into the experiential realm with God.

---

*The spirit of revelation always hits the heart first, and then the heart teaches the mind and brings you into the experiential realm with God.*

---

I believe that this is why Jesus' message in abiding was one of the very last ones he taught His disciples right before He was crucified. If we abide in Him, we will be gloriously fruitful. *We will produce fruit even out of season*.

In fact, in Jesus' final week of ministry before His crucifixion, he spoke to a fig tree because it had leaves but no fruit. The next day, the tree withered from the roots. Fig trees typically bear leaves in the late spring to early summer, and fruit typically appears at the same time. The week Jesus was crucified, it was early spring, so it would have been too early for the tree to bear leaves or fruit (Matt 21:18-22). While it wasn't the *official* season, the presence of leaves was a specific botanical "promise" of fruit.

How could Jesus demand that a tree produce fruit *out of season*? Because Jesus Himself was there. In that measure of presence, He has the right to expect fruit in every season.

Jesus is the "Season." When the Author of Life stands before a tree, the calendar is irrelevant.

---

Jesus is the "Season."

When the Author of Life stands before a tree, the calendar is irrelevant.

---

The Psalms prophesied about a man who would be so complete, that they would be fruitful in *every season of life*: "Blessed is the man Who walks not in the counsel of the ungodly, Nor stands in the path of sinners, Nor sits in the seat of the scornful; But his delight is in the law of the Lord, And in His law he meditates day and night. He shall be like a tree Planted by the rivers of water, That brings forth its fruit in its season, Whose leaf also shall not wither; And whatever he does shall prosper." - Psalm 1:1-3 (NKJV)

Revelation 22:2 also echoes a similar theme. In the heavens, the tree of life bears twelve fruits- each tree yielding fruit *every month*. "In the middle of its street, and on either side of the river, was the tree of life, which bore twelve fruits, each tree yielding its fruit every month. The leaves of the tree were for the healing of the nations."

If we give ourselves an excuse to not be bearing fruit, you'll subconsciously give yourself the right to scream at someone in traffic, to gruffly respond to your children, or to angrily scream at your spouse just because you have "had a day."

But a fruitful life? *That* is the life that Jesus has called us to and fully equipped us for. That life is a sign and a wonder and re-presents the life of Christ to people around us in everyday situations. When someone is with you in the car, and they watch you bless someone who curses you, they will be shocked. When you're in line for a store but can wait there standing for hours with a smile on your face, the fruit of patience is on full display. When your kids can't get their math homework right, and you can gently show them where they've made a mistake, and not scream and cause a fight, gentleness is showing itself strong.

When you want to quit, but you've given your word, faithfulness as a fruit is manifested. Self-control is shown when you don't retaliate after being insulted.

Many times, I have heard Christians announce that they are in a wilderness season. If you consider that the Jewish nation wandered in the wilderness only because of their complaining and rebellion, it may not be so wise to call your season a wilderness. Jesus ended the wilderness experience when He was sent into the wilderness by the Holy Spirit and fasted for forty days. He prophetically fulfilled the forty years that the Jewish people wandered in the desert, *ending the need for any wilderness.* The promised land was a prophetic picture of the abundant life of Christ.

Jesus said that a fruitful life would be evident from one single thing: *abiding.* He said, "I am the vine, you are the branches. He who abides in Me, and I in him, bears much fruit; for without Me you can do nothing" (John 15:5). *Abiding produces fruit.* Therefore, if there is no fruit, it's from a lack of abiding.

---

*If there is no fruit, it's from a lack of abiding.*

---

If you realize that you're fruitless, that's step one of abiding. When Jesus taught on abiding in John 15, He told His disciples that they had already been pruned because they had heard the Word. John 15:3 says, "You are already clean (pruned) because of the word which I have spoken to you." If you're already pruned, the only thing you must do is enjoy the connection with the vine. Fruit is an inevitable byproduct.

In the vine parable that Jesus taught His disciples, He said that Abba Father was the vinedresser, and that He was the vine. Jesus' job isn't to inspect for fruit, but to grow branches. So, what is Abba's role as the vinedresser?

One day, I was in prayer and feeling horrible about screaming at one of my children. I had John 15 open in my bible and was praying in the spirit. At that time, I had never done a close study of abiding, and I assumed that what I had been taught in church was correct. What I had been taught was that if I didn't bear fruit, that I would be a branch cut off the vine and thrown in the fire. I cried, "Lord, I'm so sorry that I'm not fruitful. I know you're going to come and cut me off! I don't want to be cut off... I'm sorry!"

Instead, I suddenly had an open vision. I saw Abba Father, the vinedresser, begin to walk near to me. His pace was unhurried, and His movements gentle and precise. Smiling, He came towards me- the branch that was naked of fruit. Tenderly, and with all the love in the world, He reached down to my branch. I braced for the tearing away, but instead what I found was Him lifting me towards the vine and propping me closer to the core of the plant. I was shocked.

Instead of casting me, a fruitless branch, away and throwing me into a firepit, He gave me more specialized attention and drew me closer to the source of strength. After this encounter, I looked up how vinedressers deal with fruitless branches. Guess what? They always prop them up and give them more support to grow. I went back to the scriptures and read the verse again that had always troubled me: John 15:2 - "Every branch in Me that does not bear fruit He takes away; and every branch that bears fruit He prunes, that it may bear more fruit."

The words "takes away" is the word *ario* in Greek. It does not mean to throw away, rather, it means to lift towards. The Father doesn't throw away fruitless branches. *He lifts them towards Himself.*

The Father lifts (ario) the fruitless branch to give it light, and He prunes the fruitful branch to give it focus. Both actions are moved by the same hand of love—one to start the life, the other to maximize it.

One time, I heard the story of a father who had 15 children. Someone interviewing him asked, "Fifteen children- wow! Which one is your favorite?"

The father responded, "Well, today Mike had a math test he bombed. So today, he was my favorite. The day before, our little Christine fell and scraped her knee while trying to learn how to ride her bike. That day, she was my favorite. Two days ago, my older daughter Rachel bombed a job interview, and she really needed me to be there for her to pick the pieces of her heart off the floor. That day, she was my favorite."

The interviewer was shocked. "So, your favorite isn't the child with the most awards and accolades?"

"No," the father responded. "The one who is hurting the most gets the most attention- and that day is my favorite."

After my encounter with the Lord, I now feel such freedom and acceptance from the Father. He's not an angry taskmaster, who comes to inspect how good of a job I've been at producing fruit for Him. No, He's much more into focusing on the quality of connection, knowing that *focusing on the connection* will fix everything.

## The Connection Point

During a big storm in Houston one year, we lost some cell towers near us. For a few hours, I was unable to connect to my husband and let him know that we were ok. The storm was a nasty one, and I was very concerned about his safety, but also wanted him to know that we were ok. It was a very scary feeling not only for my girls and I, but also for him. That kind of fear is unlike other kinds of fear. Connection is *imperative* for relationships.

How do we focus on connection? Let's return to John 15 where Jesus teaches about the connection point to Him: abiding. The word "abide" in Greek is the word "meno." This word has single-handedly brought me into a deeper place of prayer because of its meaning. Meno means "seamless union."

Think about the clothes you're wearing right now. A t-shirt is put together usually by at least four different pieces of fabric- sewn together into one. Jeans are made from 3-4 pieces- maybe even more. They all have *seams* to make a single garment.

Interestingly, Jesus wore a garment *without seam.* "Now the tunic was without seam, woven from the top in one piece" (John 19:23-24). This garment was a very expensive garment for the time period- which is why the soldiers gambled for it. It was the Gucci garment of that day!

Why did Jesus specifically wear a garment without seam? I believe it was to model for us prophetically what the crucifixion would become for us- a place of seamless union, woven in Him. Psalm 139:13 says, "For You formed my inward parts; You knit me in my mother's womb."

Imagine for a moment what your life would look like if you believed this truth. Far from being separated from Him, He has become woven in your DNA without seam. You can't find the part where He starts, and you finish, or where you finish, and He starts. You have become *one.*

With this in mind, read 1 John 3:6. It says, "Whoever abides in Him does not sin. Whoever sins has neither seen Him nor known Him." Can you see now why an abiding life of seamless union would create a person who *does not sin?*

I'll be the first to tell you, I'm not there yet. However, the more that I spend time meditating on these truths and agreeing with these verses in prayer, I experience His power flowing through me, and I experience fruitful living more often.

There is a place of absolute rest where we can remain in seamless union abiding, allowing Him to do all the work to grow the fruit. A plant never tries and struggles to produce fruit- it is simply the product of abiding. The amazing part about this whole process is that when a fruit of the Spirit is evident in my life, I can take absolutely no credit for it, and I turn and praise and thank God, who is able to produce such a miracle!

## Jesus and the Fig Tree

I mentioned the fig tree earlier, but I want to take a little closer look at just how important that fig tree incident was.

Jesus has just made His triumphant entry into Jerusalem and entered the temple. Shouts of "Hosanna! Hosanna!" were still ringing in His ears as He walked up the steps with His disciples. He looked around and then left town and headed to Bethany (Mark 11:11-14).

## Bearing Fruit

The next morning, Jesus was headed back into Jerusalem. He was hungry and spotted a fig tree. He drew near to see if any fruit was on it.

I imagine Jesus walking up to the tree. Fig leaves are huge, and this tree had lots of them. I think of how the leaves must have blown in the wind, and I can hear the crunch of sand and dirt under Jesus' feet as he nears the tree. Looking into the tree, Jesus carefully moves the leaves around to see if there is any fruit on the tree.

What if, at this very moment, He was suddenly reminded of Adam and Eve, and their fig leaves? I wonder if He pictured them and groaned inside at the loss the fig leaves represented. They represented the day the walk in Eden stopped, and the separation began.

It was with the fig leaves that Adam and Eve tried to cover themselves out of shame. The fig leaves, with their bold large canvas, were more than big enough to do the job.

I don't believe Jesus was looking for a snack. He said plainly in other scriptures that "He had food we knew not of." I think this was a different kind of hunger- the hunger to be united again with His Bride. He was looking for the restoration of Eden. He was looking for a life that didn't need to hide.

1 Peter 4:8 says, "love covers a multitude of sin." Instead of letting God's love cover and unite Adam and Eve, they tried to cover themselves. It was a sad, cold action that was a result of Adam and Eve believing the illusion that their sin

separated them from God's love, and therefore, *from each other.*

I believe God was deeply grieved and experienced great loss when Eden, a place of fruitful abundance, was suddenly reduced to disconnected leaves. Let's take a closer look at what happened:

> *"Now the next day, when they had come out from Bethany, He was hungry. And seeing from afar a fig tree having leaves, He went to see if perhaps He would find something on it. When He came to it, He found nothing but leaves, for it was not the season for figs.*
>
> *In response Jesus said to it, "Let no one eat* **fruit** *from you ever again."" (Mark 11:13-14)*

Now what's crazy is that there's a Greek word in there that doesn't really make sense in English. Most translations smooth it over by saying "Jesus said to the tree," but the literal Greek word used is *apokritheis*, which means "to answer" or "to respond." So, what happened? The fig tree was speaking to Jesus.

If Jesus is *answering* the tree, it implies the tree was "saying" something first.

Jesus wasn't "cursing" a helpless plant (Peter thought Jesus cursed it, but that is not the case); He was responding to a lie.

The tree had leaves. In the biology of a fig tree, the small, edible buds usually appear at the same time as, or even before, the leaves. So, by having leaves, the tree was proclaiming to every hungry traveler: *"I have fruit."* It was mirroring the original "fig leaf" behavior from Eden: an outward covering to hide an internal lack.

Right after Jesus spoke to the fig tree, He headed into Jerusalem to cleanse the temple. I believe these two events are not coincidence, but they are a parable of the religious systems that Jesus came to expose.

The Pharisees could never produce fruit. All they wanted was to check boxes to say they had "served" God by their performance or efforts. They checked all the boxes of the law, but their hearts were calloused and void of love. They gave money but did not understand generosity. They prayed long prayers, but it was for show. They craved authority and power, but they were full of insecurity. *They were fruitless, and Jesus knew it.*

The Pharisees were the architects of a system made of leaves. They offered the world a grand canopy of religious activity, but like the tree, their 'temple' had become a marketplace of effort rather than a house of abiding. Jesus wasn't just clearing furniture; He was answering a system that had become a barrier to the very fruit it was meant to produce.

*This leads us to a hard, necessary diagnostic:*

**Which tree is in you?**

## Which Tree Is In You?

At the very beginning of the human story, there were two trees in the Garden: the Tree of Life and the Tree of the Knowledge of Good and Evil. One tree represented truth and abundance. The other tree represented the catastrophic results of believing a lie. One offered life through dependence on God; the other offered a life of independence, judgment, and "performance."

Thousands of years after Adam and Eve ate of the fruit of the Knowledge of Good and Evil, John the Baptist arrived to announce the return of Messiah.

When John the Baptist began to preach a message of repentance, he issued a startling warning to the Pharisees who were listening and watching him: "And even now the axe is laid to the root of the trees" (Matthew 3:10).

For years, I thought this was a threat of judgment against people. Honestly, it made me scared that God was going to cut me down!

But looking through the lens of the "incorruptible seed," I see something much more beautiful. Trees in scripture are constantly used as parables of ways of thinking. Jesus didn't come to chop down *people*; He came to put an axe to the root of that old system—the Tree of the Knowledge of Good and Evil.

The Tree of the Knowledge of Good and Evil was present, but it wasn't a problem until Adam and Eve ate it and began to partake of its fruit. It was their thinking that led to the action of eating. "Did God really say...?"

People's actions have never been the problem.

Ways of thinking have been the problem.

The Tree of Knowledge represents the root of "good" works done in our own strength and "bad" works that lead to shame. It is the tree of "I should," "I must," and "I failed," and "I have to try harder."

The Tree of Life wasn't lost in Eden; it was hidden in a Person. When Jesus stood before that fig tree, the Tree of Life was 'answering' the tree of religious effort.

As Jesus hung on the tree called "the cross," He was declaring an end to that old system of law and self-effort. The only thing *that* tree could produce was death- but He came to bring life! Jesus reversed the curse.

In the final chapter of the Bible, the Tree of Knowledge is nowhere to be found. *Only the Tree of Life remains.*

*"In the middle of its street, and on either side of the river, was the tree of life, which bore twelve fruits, each tree yielding its fruit every month. The leaves of the tree were for the healing of the nations." —Revelation 22:2*

If we are in "seamless union" with Christ, then Revelation 22 is a not a paradigm for a future, distant city; it is a reality of your new interior life. *The new Eden inside of you.*

**The River:** The Holy Spirit flowing from your innermost being (John 7:38).

**The Tree**: Christ, the Vine, rooted in your heart (John 14).

**The Twelve Fruits:** A constant, monthly supply of His nature—patience for January, joy for February, peace for March—regardless of the "season" of life you're in.

**The Healing Leaves:** Instead of the leaves symbolizing shame that we cover ourselves with, our lives of abiding produce healing to those around us.

If the Garden has been restored within us, we have to ask a dangerous question: How do we actually partake of its life?

In Eden, the fall wasn't just a bad decision. We literally ate our way into separation by partaking of a fruit that promised independence but delivered death. It was bad fruit! To reverse this, Jesus didn't just give us a lecture to try harder to measure up. He invited us a Table.

When Jesus told the crowds in John 6 that they must 'eat His flesh and drink His blood,' He was inviting them into a new paradigm.

Have you ever been a bit put off that Jesus wanted people to eat His flesh and drink His blood? I know it becomes cultural to accept this, but considering what we've learned, perhaps there is another way to view what Jesus actually said.

In Aramaic, the language Jesus spoke, the word for flesh is *besra*. In Aramaic tradition, this isn't just a word for human skin; it is the exact same word used for the flesh or pulp of a fruit. Jesus was identifying Himself as the Tree of Life, but He was also honoring the law of creation He established in Genesis 1: *that every fruit has its seed within itself.*

When Jesus held up the bread and the wine—the fruit of the grain and the fruit of the vine—He was showing us that the very life of the Father was now available for us to consume. He wasn't just giving us a religious ritual; He was identifying Himself as the Tree of Life.

Think about the architecture of a piece of fruit. The *besra* (the flesh) is what we taste and consume, but the seed is hidden at the very center of that flesh. You don't get to the seed unless you eat of the flesh of the fruit.

When we partake of the 'flesh' of Jesus—His broken body and His sacrificed life—we aren't just getting a temporary meal. We are taking in the fruitful life of Christ! We taste and then see that He is good! Because the seed is *in* the fruit, when you eat of Him, His life (love in its many forms: joy, peace, patience, goodness, faithfulness and self-control) is reproduced in yours. You don't have to 'try' to act like Jesus any more than an apple tree 'tries' to make apples. By eating the Fruit of His life, the DNA of the Vine is planted in the soil of your heart.

This is what it means to be a 'partaker of the divine nature' (2 Peter 1:4). The word partaker in the Greek is *koinonos*, which means a sharer or a partner. It's the same root word for 'communion.' You aren't just a human trying to act like a Christian; you have been given a seat at the table of His very essence. When you partake of the *besra* (the pulp) of His life, you aren't just getting 'help' for your day—you are *receiving the actual nature of God.*

You cannot 'think' your way into a new nature. You can't feel that conviction you did something wrong and then pull on your boots and muscle it up. (fruit doesn't have any muscle fibers to flex!) Instead, you must partake of it.

This is why Jesus instituted Communion *before* He was crucified. He was providing the 'user manual' for His own crushing. He wasn't a victim; He was the Vinedresser overseeing the release of the Seed. Just as a grape must be crushed to release the wine, Jesus' *besra* had to be broken to release the Spirit into our lives.

In Eden, we ate our way out of the Presence. At the Table, we eat our way back into the Person. We don't just stand *near* the Tree of Life anymore; we become the very ground where that Tree grows. The 'Meno' (seamless union) is complete: His life becomes our life, reproduced by the power of the Seed that remains in us.

The axe has been laid to the old root of the law of performance. You are no longer judged by how well you are "doing." You no longer must eat from the tree of "Am I good enough today?" Instead, you simply lean back into the seamless union and receive from the Tree of Life.

Think back to the very moment Adam and Eve were sent out of Eden. We've often been taught that God stationed an angel with a flaming sword as a terrifying guard to keep us out. It always made me shake with fear that if someone ever came close to those swords they would die. But if you look at the Hebrew meaning, a different meaning entirely emerges.

The word for 'keep' is *shamar*—to preserve and cherish. The 'sword' was not a weapon of war! It was placed there to keep the way back to the Tree of Life. God wasn't hiding the path to keep evil people out. *He was lighting it.* That flaming presence at the gate was the first 'lighthouse' of history.

It was God saying, 'I am preserving the road home. I am keeping the way open until the Seed can be planted and the Table can be set.' Can you picture the Father and prodigal son in this image? The Father has always had His arms open and waiting for us.

You don't have to wait for Heaven to experience Revelation 22. Because His seed remains in you, the Garden has been restored within.

The question is no longer "How hard are you working?" but rather, "Which tree is in you?

# CHAPTER THREE

# How to Really Be "In Love."

When I first began dating my husband, I thought about him all the time. I wanted to be with him more often, call him and speak to him longer, and spend as much time as I could with him. We did everything together. We rode our bikes every evening after work and worked on projects together on the weekends. We cooked meals, painted walls, and helped me install lights in my townhome. When we met, my husband was studying for his FE engineering exam. An FE exam is what engineers need to pass to be able to stamp drawings- much like passing the Bar exam for a lawyer. That went out the window! We were *in love.*

I'm sure you can relate to a time when you were in love. Dating relationships always start off with batting eyes, being enthralled with one another, and thinking you've found perfection in another human. However, time goes on, and about half of marriages that began "in love" eventually fail and fall apart. How is this possible?

1 Cor 13:8 tells us that love does not fail. If it failed, *it must have not truly been love.*

God is love, (1 John 4:8) so it is safe to say that two people who have their lives fully given over to God cannot fail in a marriage. The statistics for marriage failures are just about the same in Christian vs. non-Christian homes, so what is the missing piece of the puzzle?

Perhaps, we don't know the depths of the in-love dimension.

There are between 361 and 551 times (depending on the translation) that the word "love" is mentioned in the Bible. In the Old Testament, it's mentioned 131 times, but in the New Testament, a whopping 250 times. The Old Testament has 929 chapters, being the much larger section of our Bibles. The New Testament only has 260 chapters. That means that not only is the word love mentioned more often, but for every 9 chapters of the Old Testament you would read, you would see the word love once. However, for every single chapter in the New Testament, you see the word love *in every chapter*.

We are introduced to the fact that God is love (1 John 4:7) by John the beloved, the only apostle who was not martyred (Multiple times, authorities tried to murder him but failed). John was the only one who addressed himself by, "the one whom Jesus loved" (John 13:23, John 19:26, John 20:2, John 21:7, John 21:20). It's one thing to be loved by God, but it's something else entirely to introduce yourself as the one whom God loves.

I believe John touched something that is available to all of us, but few choose to lean in and receive: the deep, all-encompassing accepting love of God. There were 12 disciples that Jesus called, but only John took the love that was offered, and let it *reidentify him.* Love identifies what God inherently is, rather than an action he performs. Because John was able to accept this, he *became* it.

If God just 'did' love, He could stop doing it. But because He IS love, He cannot stop being Himself toward you.

John wasn't being arrogant; he was being responsive. He was the only one who leaned his head on Jesus' chest. He took the "closest seat" available. Identity always precedes activity.

The concept of being "in love" is referenced 19 times in the New Testament. Here are a few of those instances:

- Ephesians 1:4: *"Just as He chose us in Him before the foundation of the world, that we should be holy and without blame before Him in love."*
- Ephesians 3:17-19: "*That Christ may dwell in your hearts through faith; that you, being rooted and grounded in love, may be able to comprehend with all the saints what is the width and length and depth and height—to know the love of Christ which passes knowledge; that you may be filled with all the fullness of God."*
- Ephesians 4:2: "*With all lowliness and gentleness, with longsuffering, bearing with one another in love."*
- Ephesians 4:15-16: "*But, speaking the truth in love, may grow up in all things into Him who is the head—Christ—from whom the whole body, joined and knit together by what every joint supplies, according to the effective working by which every part does its share, causes growth of the body for the edifying of itself in love."*
- Colossians 2:2: "*That their hearts may be encouraged, being knit together in love, and attaining to all riches of the full assurance of understanding, to the knowledge of the mystery of God, both of the Father and of Christ."*
- 1 John 4:16: "*And we have known and believed the love that God has for us. God is love, and he who abides in love abides in God, and God in him."*

- 1 John 4:18: "*There is no fear in love; but perfect love casts out fear, because fear involves torment. But he who fears has not been made perfect in love.*"

Did you notice that every single one of these verses speaks about how we relate to God and to others? ***Love is the bond of perfection.***

Colossians 3:12-15 says, "*Therefore, as the elect of God, holy and beloved, put on tender mercies, kindness, humility, meekness, longsuffering; bearing with one another, and forgiving one another, if anyone has a complaint against another; even as Christ forgave you, so you also must do.* ***But above all these things put on love, which is the bond of perfection.***"

We can be holy, beloved, be tender, have kindness, and other fruit of the spirit, but Paul emphasizes the source of all the fruit: *love*.

Can you imagine if scientists discovered a perfect bonding agent that never wore out or gave up? An agent that could withstand the test of time? They would be millionaires! People have a created desire within themselves to have lasting products. God has put eternity into the heart of man (Ecc. 3:11), and that desire can only be fulfilled inside of perfect, accepting love.

One night, I attended a service and there was a special speaker ministering. It was a Saturday evening, and the church was absolutely packed. I remember sitting in the audience, and the palpable love of God began to fill the atmosphere as he preached.

He did an altar call near the end of the service, and I'm pretty sure the entire congregation got out of their seats and ran to the front. It was packed up there! Standing room only, we were shoulder to shoulder. The minister was walking near to where I was standing but there were still about four people away from me. He put his hand on a man, and he immediately fell backwards in the spirit. All the people around that were close enough to touch him began to fall like a wave- not because the man fell on them, but because the Spirit fell. The guy that fell touched a man that was in front of a woman that was in front of me. Her shoulder briefly touched mine, and a zap of lighting love filled me. I stood there *shocked.*

The presence of God had traveled through four people to get to me, and it still had enough power to move me. If you've never had something like this happen to you, it's very difficult to explain. Sometimes, when things like that happen that you have no bible verse for or framework for, but you know it was so Holy and so powerful, your head just spins.

The next morning was Sunday morning, and we arrived at church as usual. I remember distinctly walking into the church building filled with people that I knew. Some of these people I didn't really get along with very well, and some I barely knew, and some I really liked. But that morning, I walked in, and I was *overwhelmed* with love for each person I saw. I felt so silly, but I literally cried and hugged every person who came in my path. I've never experienced anything like it before or since. However, having experienced it briefly, I know that it's possible to feel a high degree of God's love towards *every single person*. That day, I didn't care if I didn't "like" someone very well. I loved them too deeply, and it broke every other barrier. I *experienced* the bond of perfection.

When we embrace love as the supreme and perfect bond, we begin to see our relationships in a new light. This Godly love transcends human limitations, enabling us to forgive, endure, and cherish relationships. By anchoring ourselves in the love of Christ and recognizing the true source of our conflicts, we are equipped to nurture deeper, more resilient connections with those around us. Love is not just an ethereal concept but a powerful, transformative force that empowers God's nature in us, and binds us together in perfect unity.

# CHAPTER FOUR

# Spiritual Warfare in Relationships

I remember like it was yesterday- my pastor was standing on the stairs of the altar, holding up his arm. He took the fingers of his other hand and punched the skin of his arm. It was the first year my husband and I were married, and we fought a lot. My husband is from Ecuador, and I'm from Iowa. The vast cultural difference was one thing, but the spiritual aspects of our marriage were quite another. He grew up Catholic, and I was raised Baptist. We fought, and we fought a lot.

With his arm raise in the air, my pastor said, "Now you guys go ahead and raise up your arm and pinch it. Now, if your spouse is sitting next to you, grab their arm and pinch it. Do you know what that is? *It's flesh and blood.* Let me introduce you to a verse: "For our struggle is not against flesh and blood, but against the rulers, against the authorities, against the powers of this dark world and against the spiritual forces of evil in the heavenly realms" (Eph. 6:12).

My jaw hit the floor. I thought for sure that my fight was against my husband. That day, the spirit of revelation hit me in the head, and I realized for the first time that the battle I was in had nothing to do with my husband but had everything to do with powers of darkness. Demons are real, and they whisper to you, "be offended" or "just quit" or "my husband is always wrong" or "it will always be like this. Its hopeless."

People are not the enemy. What the devil will do is use us to target one another, hoping to disguise himself in the fray of bitterness and unforgiveness. If you take the devil's bait, you will aim your weapon in the wrong direction and end up hurting others and yourself in the process.

This one revelation helped me begin to see past what my husband was doing to me, and I could begin to see the man who was being tormented by demonic voices and accusations. Instead of accusation, compassion began to grow in my heart.

When we understand that our fight is *never* with people, but it's with evil thoughts, it helps to change our perspective on some things. Although there are evil spirits, the battle that we are in is not this evenly matched tennis match where the devil wins some matches, and God wins some matches. No! Satan was defeated in Christ's work on the cross. Hebrews 2:14 says, "Since the children have flesh and blood, he too shared in their humanity so that by his death he might break the power of him who holds the power of death—that is, the devil."

The power of the devil *has been broken.*

Colossians 2:15 says, *"And having disarmed the powers and authorities, he made a public spectacle of them, triumphing over them by the cross."*

The word "disarmed" in the Greek is the word *apekduomai.* It's translated from two words- *apo,* which means away from, and *ekduo,* to be stripped of clothing: to disarm. Any weapons that satan and his demon army carried were confiscated that day. The Mirror Translation remarks, "He (Jesus) stripped all the spiritual tyrants in the universe of their sham authority at the Cross and marched them naked through the streets."

When Jesus died on the cross, He descended into Hell and took captivity captive. He regained the authority that Adam gave away when he ate the apple, and with those keys, rose victoriously! "I am He who lives, and was dead, and behold,

I am alive forevermore. Amen. And I have the keys of Hades and of Death" (Rev. 1:18).

During the three days He was dead, Jesus stripped the demons naked. Demons don't wear clothes, so what were they stripped naked of? Their weapons. The only weapons they had were the weapons Adam and Eve laid down when they ate the fruit in the garden. Jesus as the second Adam won back the rights that the first Adam left lying on the ground.

The enemy is now weaponless. All he has at his disposal is a taunting voice with no real power.

The enemy's only weapon left is deception. Since he has no sword, he has to convince *us* to pick up his old demonic weapons (anger, slander) and use them on each other.

The spirit realm is real. Demons are real and Holy Spirit is real, but the sword fight is over. Jesus won! Now all that's left to do is to pick up the weapons that He purchased for us- the sword of the Spirit. Colossians 2:10 says, "... and you are complete in Him, who is the head of all principality and power." We have been completely empowered for victory! With Jesus as *the head* of all principalities and power, and us finding ourselves IN Him, we can walk in total victory!

Colossians 1:13 says, *"He has delivered us from the power of darkness and conveyed us into the kingdom of the Son of His love..."* Did you notice that the verse says, "He has *delivered?"* It's past tense. It already happened!

Some days, it may not feel like we are walking in total victory in Christ. What is the missing link? We must understand that *Holy Spirit* is the one spirit that destroys all opposing spirits. Satan is defeated, but he isn't dead. We need to learn to walk in the victory in Christ that we already have.

Phil 1:27-28 reads, *"... you stand fast in one Spirit, with one mind striving together for the faith of the gospel, and not in any way terrified by your adversaries, which is to them a proof of perdition, but to you of salvation, and that from God"*

The unity of the Holy Spirit in God's people produces a single mind. Holy Spirit helps us all think the way that God thinks- and one of these ways is that we are *not in any way terrified* of the adversary! If you are afraid in any way that the devil is going to "get you" for something, it's allowed to remain because the Spirit has not yet taught you about the finished work of Christ. Not only is the devil defeated, but Paul cranks it up a notch when he says that when we have no fear, it is evidence we have fully embraced the gospel.

When the Church begins to believe the devil is absolutely, utterly, totally defeated, it is *proof of our salvation*!

It's no wonder, because *perfect love casts out all fear.* Love is spiritual warfare!

Having the Holy Spirit brings a unity to the Church that is impossible without it. If the devil can bring division with spirits, how much more can Holy Spirit bring unity? Paul prayed for his Philippian church that they would have the *same love* that he felt towards them. "Therefore, if there is any consolation in Christ, if any comfort of love, if any fellowship of the Spirit, if any affection and mercy, fulfill my joy by being like-minded, having the same love, being of one accord of one mind" (Phil 2:1-2).

Have you been feeling like there is spiritual warfare in a relationship in your life? Remember, we aren't wrestling against flesh and blood. The cross of Christ has finished all the work! Love is now a fruit that is abundantly available, and unity comes to the church when the fruit of love is visibly evident. Love casts out all fear of fighting with people, because they are flesh and blood, and we don't wrestle with flesh and blood! The same love that Paul had for his churches, we can have for the church.

---

*Unity comes to the church when the fruit of love is visibly evident.*

---

## Satan Can't Cast Out Satan

My daughter Abby was sitting quietly on her bed, working hard on her English when her sister, Makayla, burst into the room with our dog, Togo. Loudly announcing her arrival, Makayla rushed in and crashed into Abby's bed with the dog right on her heels. In a split second, there were two people and a big bundle of fur on the bed. Togo stepped on the computer on Abby's lap, and she frustratedly screamed, "*Makayla*!" Makayla immediately screamed back, "*Abby*! I was just coming in to have some fun!" She fumed and stomped out of the room and slammed her door, indignant that her sister didn't welcome her into her room.

Sound like something that has happened in your home? It happens in my house all the time! Our immediate, knee-jerk response to anger is usually always to be angry. It's culturally normal, even in Christian homes.

But what if there were a different way? What if there was a way to respond like Christ?

*In* Christ, we can flip anger into kindness. Not only can we- but we must. Anger will only ever fuel more anger, causing an escalation and hurt feelings in every relationship.

How do we avoid the reaction, and respond in kindness and stop the cycle? There is a way!

In Matthew 12:24-28, some Pharisees accused Jesus of casting out demons by the power of Beelzebub, the prince of demons. In response, Jesus said, *"Every kingdom divided against itself will be ruined, and every city or household divided against itself will not stand." If Satan drives out Satan, he is divided against himself. How then can his kingdom stand? And if I drive out demons by Beelzebul, by whom do your people drive them out? So then, they will be your judges. But if it is by the Spirit of God that I drive out demons, then the kingdom of God has come upon you."*

Here's what Jesus meant: you cannot use a demonic weapon against a demon attack and expect it to work. *Satan can't cast out satan!*

Paul lists demonic weapons in Galatians 5:19-21: hatred, discord, jealousy, idolatry, witchcraft, fits of rage, selfish ambition, envy, and so on. We could add in flattery, coercion, blame, slander, blackmail, backbiting, accusation or throwing someone under the bus.

---

*In relational conflicts, you cannot use a demonic weapon and expect to bring about a Kingdom result.*

---

In relational conflicts, you *cannot* use a demonic weapon and expect to bring about a Kingdom result. Just like my daughters modeled, anger will produce anger. You can't use anger to overturn disobedience. You can't use manipulation to try and resolve division. You can't overturn a harsh word with another harsh word. A demonic weapon will never bring about healing or peace.

Let me make this practical: if someone angrily screams at you, screaming back to them will only produce more demonic activity. The *soft word* is the only response that stops the anger cycle. I'm sure you've tried it countless times- I have, too. Screaming never works. I'm not sure why we always think we must be louder than the person we are arguing with for them to hear us. Scripture says that the one who speaks *softest* will be the one to change the spirit of the conversation.

Need another example? If your child is disobedient, and you angrily yell at them and tell them to go to their room, do they walk gently away and sweetly say, "love you?" No, usually they stomp off down the hallway and slam the door. Anger produced anger.

Here's what's fascinating about Jesus' discussion with the Pharisees- He specifically said that by the *Spirit of God,* demons would be driven out. Jesus didn't drive out the demons alone. The Holy Spirit and Jesus worked *together*. When we operate in the kingdom, we operate in unity because any power we have comes from the Holy Spirit who dwells within us. That means there are two agreeing- and where two or more agree concerning any one thing, it will be done for them (Matt. 18:19).

---

*Any power we have comes from the Holy Spirit who dwells within us.*

---

The place of agreement and unity with God is the only place that there is power to cast out demons.

In the Kingdom, we have the ability through the Holy Spirit to overturn a harsh word with a kind word. If someone hates us, we have been empowered to return love. Proverbs 15:1 says, "A gentle answer turns away wrath, but a harsh word stirs up anger."

The next time you're tempted to return anger for anger with your spouse, or correct a child roughly, remember that God has empowered you through His Spirit to operate in the opposite spirit! Overturn that harsh word with a kind word.

Choose to say nothing if the other person is mean. Actively look for ways to bless those who treat you wrongly.

## Relational Conflict

Most people know very well about conflict with others, and it's become a normal part of their lives. What they don't understand, however, is to go through that conflict and find peace and resolution on the other side of the conflict.

I was listening to a teaching once, and the teacher suddenly said, "Why can't we fight with our friends the way we fight with our spouses?" I got what he meant immediately. My husband and I have had our share of ugly, screaming fights. Yes, I said it- it's happened on many occasions. We don't, however, see those kinds of disagreements and fights between friendships. Why? Because most of the time, "christianese" culture will just slowly back away from the person, and find another friend to invest in. They move on from the friendship, because it gets difficult.

One major fight, and the friendship disappears.

What's the problem with that? In hoping from friendship to friendship, we rob ourselves of the privilege of being corrected, and thus beautifully refined by love. The conflict that took place likely took place in an area where you or the other person needed some refining in understanding. If you subvert the process simply by ending the painful relationship, that transformation can never take place! When conflict arises, the best thing you could possibly do is to sit in prayer and begin to ask Holy Spirit to show you where *you* went wrong.

---

*When conflict arises, the best thing you could possibly do is to sit in prayer and begin to ask Holy Spirit to show you where you went wrong.*

---

Holy Spirit is not shy about bringing corrections. There's never been a time that He hasn't shown me my part in what I've done wrong and released the grace to walk in forgiveness- and for my part, reconciliation.

There have been times that I have needed to part ways with people. It was a good thing for both of us, and when we went our separate ways, were still able to both prosper and share the gospel. Neither of us turned bitter or resentful but respected one another from a distance. The separation of Paul and Barnabas in Acts 15:36-41 is a perfect example of this. They chose to have mutual respect and were able to move in different directions without slandering, publicly ridiculing, or stoning each other to death.

But... sometimes it doesn't go like that. Sometimes, the stones get thrown as one person tries to walk away from a relationship. Most often, that happens because of jealousy. We see it often in the New Testament- specifically between

Jesus and the Pharisees, and then the Apostles and the Pharisees after Jesus' resurrection.

What do we do when religious leaders or brothers throw stones? Consider what Stephen went through in the book of Acts. Stephen was a man that as described as being full of faith and power and did many wonders and signs. (Acts 6:8). Stephen had such wisdom by the Holy Spirit; jealousy was stirred up from a group of Jews from the Synagogue of the Freedmen.

The Synagogue of the Freedmen (also known as the Synagogue of the Libertines) was a group of Hellenistic Jews in Jerusalem. The term "freedmen" refers to Jews who were once slaves or prisoners of Rome and had been freed. These individuals, along with others from regions like Cyrene, Alexandria, Cilicia, and Asia, settled in Jerusalem and formed this synagogue. These people still had a slavery mentality, and they could not stand hearing Stephen teach or preach on freedom in Christ.

The Freedmen stirred up the elders, scribes and people that Stephen was serving, and set up false witnesses against him. They bring Stephen to a council of Jewish elders, and it's there that Stephen preaches to High Priest an Israeli history lesson (Acts 7-8). In that history lesson, Stephen specifically points out that the leaders that chose to reject God and killed the prophets were "stiff-necked and uncircumcised in heart and ears! *You always resist the Holy Spirit...*" (Acts 7:51).

Do you remember what happened when Peter preached a beautiful message at Pentecost, empowered by Holy Spirit? 3,000 people were "cut to the heart" and *saved* that day

(Acts 2:37-41). However, when the Holy Spirit is resisted, that same power that cuts to the heart produces a *murderous spirit*. As Stephen finished his history/sermon, Acts 7:54 says, "When they (the pharisees) heard these things, they were *cut to the heart*, and they gnashed at him with their teeth."

What Stephen did next is one of my favorite pieces of scripture. "*But he, being full of the Holy Spirit, gazed into heaven and saw the glory of God, and Jesus standing at the right hand of God" (Acts 7:55).*

As the jealous, religious Pharisees were throwing stones, the Holy Spirit empowered Stephen to be able to maintain a place of beholding God. Stephen wasn't looking at the charges filed against him, or his death sentence, but was lost in beholding God's glory. He wasn't stuck trying to defend himself, he didn't justify his message, and from that point on, he didn't say a word to the Pharisees.

While they stoned him to death, Stephen fixed his gaze heavenward in prayer.

He became what he beheld. Stephen's eyes were locked on the heavens- on the Man who had gone before Him and made a way for him to follow. Stephen saw victorious Jesus, standing at the right hand of the Father after He suffered much. He knew that God alone holds the power of life and death, and He looked to the only one who could raise Him and empower him. The pressure that was put on Stephen in that moment revealed what was inside of him: God's Holy Spirit, empowering him with the meekness of the Lamb of God.

Because he was a man of prayer, and a man who beheld God's glory, Stephen was able to say the same words that Jesus spoke on the cross, as he died for a sin he never committed. He said, "Lord Jesus, receive my spirit," and "Lord, do not charge them with this sin."

If someone is attacking you, slandering your character, speaking evilly of you, and trying to excommunicate you, you don't need to defend yourself. Instead of responding to accusations or trying to defend yourself, spend your time and energy beholding Jesus.

Literally, let God be your defender.

---

*Let God be your defender.*

---

If you ever have a time in your life that a leader or brother or sister wants to stone you and cast you out, take Stephen as an example to follow. Keep your eyes fixated on Christ. Behold His ability to pray amid extreme suffering and persecution. Let mercy be on your tongue as you ask the Father not to charge them with the sin they've committed against you. Pray for them until the pain has passed, and love for them begins to flow.

If you choose to not take the conflict to prayer, chances are... not only is the relationship is over, but you will live with a wound called "church hurt." Many then draw back from the church, never to join another group. Prayer is the "debriding" of the wound. Just like a physical wound needs to be cleaned so it doesn't get infected, prayer cleans the "stones" out of our hearts so they don't turn into bitterness.

This hurt can impact not only your ability to have someone lead you, but all the other relationships you have in your life. If you do not have a prayer life at all, the truth is your marriage and friendships will greatly struggle. They simply cannot thrive in a prayerless environment. Ask any man or woman whose spouse does not pray, and they will tell you about deep levels of unresolved conflict over decades. The pain builds up to such a hard place, they have impenetrable walls guarding their hearts from further damage. The fact that they are still married on paper does not mean that the marriage they have is God's highest or best.

The Holy Spirit doesn't just want to save your marriage license; He wants to restore the 'in-love' dimension that makes the marriage a joy.

Your prayer life fuels all intimate relationships. To have any intimacy with your spouse, it is imperative that both of you hear from Holy Spirit, and that you both are moving forward in the direction of wisdom and understanding.

This doesn't just apply to marriages. This applies to friendships as well. The strongest friendships I have are the friendships that have been rooted in the place of prayer. We have each worked through the conflict, willing to learn where each one of us went wrong. In times of conflict with my closest friends, I can count on the fact that *both* of us are running to our prayer closets first to resolve the conflict. It is *so* reassuring to know that both of us are working together towards achieving reconciliation and peace.

In the friendships I have walked this out with, the breakthrough after the storm is the sweetest place of closeness. The fellowship and the love that I have experienced with these friends takes on a new richness. In fact, the most profound experiences in the love of God I have tangibly experienced have been in *these* friendships.

You must use careful discernment in the place of prayer to ask Holy Spirit about the relationship in which you're experiencing conflict. He will show you if it's a Paul and Barnabas separation, a Stephen stoning, or covenant friendship that will last for a lifetime.

# CHAPTER FIVE

# Born of God

Two orphan brothers came by ship to the USA from Holland 4 generations ago. One of them was my great- great- great- great grandfather, Arie Boscaljon. I can never know my distant relative personally, and I have no idea of what kind of man he was. Although I have his genetics, the time and space create an uncrossable chasm.

I used to carry the same idea in my heart as it relates to Father God. I saw Him as a great- great- great- great grandfather, thinking it was impossible to ever really know Him because of time and space. The expansive gap seemed to be impassable, and instead of bringing unity and oneness to my heart concerning God, it brought separation and distance.

Before we can explore unity within the church at a deeper level, we must first understand the closeness and belonging that a Father has to their children. This journey we are going to go on is a two-part journey: our personal relationship with God, and then our relationship with others in the family of God. Family is the word that will be used often, because more than anything, God wanted to create an expansion of His family in the earth.

Every family has a mother and father. In Psalm 102, there's a name of God in verse 24 that is highlighted: "Father of Eternity." The second portion of Psalm 102 is entirely focused on the generations. Although we view generations as far apart, how does God, as Father of Eternity, view them?

The Bible rarely ever mentions grandchildren, or great grandchildren. Most of the time, entire nations were named after their father. For generations, Jews called Abraham their father. In addition, even though there were fourteen generations between King David and Jesus; Jesus was still called the *son of* David. According to the way we speak, we would say Jesus was the great-great-great- great... well, you get the idea. Fourteen greats later, we would say "grandson," of David, not even son!

This tells me that God thinks very differently about generations than we do. He sees a very close association with a father that we don't understand in our culture. Unlike the huge gap in years I have with Arie Boscaljon, God sees no distance in time from Father to son.

Romans 8:16 says, "The Spirit Himself bears witness with our spirit that we are children of God." If you are not convinced that God sees you directly as His child, perhaps the problem is that the Holy Spirit has not yet revealed it to your spirit. It is the Holy Spirit's job to make God's fatherhood something we experience daily!

---

*"You are already God's beloved child!"*

---

You are not just God's great- great- great distant grandchild, but a real *child of God.* Perhaps that's a phrase we have thrown around so long in Christianity that it's lost its real meaning. Think about your own children. Your child is your flesh and blood, and the deep bond that exists between you and your child is simply not found in other relationships. You would do anything to provide for their needs. To shelter them, clothe them, care for their heart and provide for them are easy. I will even die for my children if it means that they will live.

1 John 4:4 says, *"You are of God, little children, and have overcome...", and 1 John 3:2 adds, "beloved, we are God's*

*children right now..."* We are born of God, and He sees us as His children- *right now*!

Always keep in mind as we read the Old Testament that we must find the Gospel. Let's see if we can find Jesus in this verse: Psalm 102:18 says, "This will be written for the generation to come, that a people yet to be created may praise the Lord."

"*A people yet to be created.*" That phrase has always stood out to me. On the surface, it's about future generations — children not yet born. But Scripture loves a double meaning, and I don't think David's words stop there. The same God who creates a generation can re-create a person. 2 Corinthians 5:17 tells us, "If anyone is in Christ, he is a new creation; old things have passed away; behold, all things have become new." The people "yet to be created" aren't only the ones who haven't been born — they're also the ones, like you and me, who get to be born again.

Let's skip forward to get some New Testament context. A pharisee named Nicodemus went to Jesus at night and said to him, "Rabbi, we know that You are a teacher come from God; for no one can do these signs that You do unless God is with him." (John 3:2). Nicodemus saw Jesus as a good teacher because of the signs He did but could not see Him as anything else.

Jesus replied, "Most assuredly, I say to you, unless one is born again, he *cannot see* the kingdom of God." (John 3:3). Here is where we get our very popular phrase, "born again," but what does it mean to be "born again"?

The Message Translation translates verse 3 like this: *"Jesus answered him emphatically; no one would even be able to recognize anything as coming from God's domain unless they are born from above to begin with. The very fact that it is possible to perceive that I am in union with God, as a human being, reveals mankind's genesis from above."*

The word "again" in the phrase 'born again' in Greek is the word "anothen", and it means: from above, from the first, or from the beginning.

This 'born again' experience is a spiritual awakening to an eternal reality. As Ephesians 1:4 reminds us, He chose us in Him before the foundation of the world. This means that before you ever took a physical breath, you were a divine thought in the mind of the Father. You weren't an accident of biology; you were an intentional plan of God. Being 'born from above' isn't just a restart of your life; it's finally becoming who God always envisioned you to be before time began.

Once you realize by the Holy Spirit that God is your real Father, it completely closes the generational gap and the feeling of being very far away from Him. God is not a distant Father, but just like the prodigal son's Father, He waits for us back at the homestead to come home to His arms.

---

*God is not a distant Father, but just like the prodigal son's Father, He waits for us back at the homestead to come home to His arms.*

---

Nicodemus could not understand this spiritual reality. Can you see the kingdom of God now? Do you see that you are truly born of God, the Father of Eternity? You belong to a family that is already established, and you've found your home in the arms of the One who begot you.

## Self- Made Man vs Sonship

As long as I can remember, I have always wanted to love God and be in right relationship with Him. From my early years on, I can remember moments where I would earnestly desire to do the right thing. But desiring to do the right thing and then actually doing the right thing are two different realities.

One of those times was about five years ago. I was doing a daily Bible reading plan, and the reading for the day was Exodus 29. I came across the scriptures where it talked about Aaron and his sons consecrating themselves to be priests unto the Lord. I read about how they had to clean themselves, make the sacrifices, and wear specific clothes. One of the specific instructions stood out to me more than the others: a verse that said that they had to do a total fast for ten days before they would be ordained as official priests.

Having the desire to do the right thing, equipped with a partial understanding that we are a priesthood, I decided to consecrate myself like Aaron had done, and fast for ten days so that I could be a priest unto the Lord, too. I did it with a pure heart, but with very little understanding.

The result of my ten-day water only fast was a skin condition called dermatographia that is incredibly irritating that I still have today. My body was put under so much stress from not having enough food that my body physically reacted in a very negative way.

For years, I could not figure out how my "obeying God" could ever result with sickness.

It's only in the last few years that I have really understood what happened. My desire was right- but the process was wrong. In fasting, I was trying to *make myself into* a consecrated priest. At the core of it, I was *trying to earn and work my way* as a daughter in God's house. But that's not my job, it's Jesus' job. Jesus has *already finished* the work necessary for us to enter His priesthood, and the work needed for me to be a daughter.

*I was trying to remake myself, when only God can do that.*

Psalm 100:3 says, *"It is He who has made us, and not we ourselves..."*

There are more than 15,000 self-help books that are published every single year. Between 2014 and 2019, the number of books in the self-help skyrocketed – the category more than doubled in 5 years. What does this say about us as a people? We recognize there is a need to change something within ourselves, but we have no idea how to go about doing it.

We have thought that we must have the willpower, determination and strength to change ourselves. These man-made attempts just put a mask of hypocrisy on but never deal with the Pharisee within. If we are honest, our efforts never produce any lasting change. Most of the time, it leads us into either pride when we do well, or shame when our attempts fail. Both are sins.

The desire to be made new is right. The problem is most people go about seeking it – like I did- in the completely wrong way. *We cannot "do" to become.* We must become by faith what He has said we already are, and then the "doings" flow from our agreement with His words over us.

That begs the question: what are we already? We are already sons and daughters, which is the highest distinction there is in the Kingdom. When God the Father wanted to put Jesus on display, He said, "This is my beloved Son, in whom I am well pleased." It wasn't savior, servant, healer that the Father pointed out. It was relational sonship.

To know who we are, we must know the One who designed us. Jeremiah 1:5 declares that God knew us before He ever formed us in the womb. This speaks of the staggering depth of God's foreknowledge. In the same way an architect 'sees' a finished building before the first stone is laid, the Father 'saw' you, loved you, and predestined you to be His own long before you entered the realm of time. You were conceived in His heart before you were conceived in the earth.

Eph. 1:4-5 reads, *"For He chose us in Him before the creation of the world to be holy and blameless in His sight. In love He predestined us to be adopted as His sons through Jesus Christ, in accordance with His pleasure and will."*

The word "adoption" in that verse is a weak translation. Typically, "adopted to be His son" is misunderstood as adoption in the modern sense. People often associate it with adopting a child from another country or through the foster care system. Many think of two parents raising a child not born to them, a child who may have been unwanted, homeless, or in an orphanage.

But that is not what the word "adopted" means at all. In Hebrew tradition, adoption is a coming of age- like a Jewish Bar Mitzvah. It speaks of a son who is in their teenage years-forming their identity.

We came from being face to face with the Father, and once we come of age and understand who He is and who we are, we return to face-to-face intimacy with Him. The word "son" there that is used is the word "huiothesia" in Greek, and it carries the idea of *genetic sameness.* This is not adoption from one set of parents to another. This is adoption of same DNA coming back to same DNA.

In Roman culture, when a father "adopted" his own son (the ceremony of *Huiothesia*), the son was given the father's signet ring and the full legal power of the father's name. It wasn't about *becoming* a son; it was about being *recognized* as a son capable of doing the Father's business.

God doesn't just bring us into the family- he RE-GENED us as genetically same creations in Christ.

2 Corinthians 5:17 tells us, "*If anyone is in Christ, he is a new creation; old things have passed away; behold, all things have become new.*"

I have amazing news for you today. God made you- you do not have to remake yourself. You do not have to fast enough, pray long enough, or worship loud enough to look like Jesus. Just believe by faith that His work is enough- the coming-of-age day has come- we have *already been regened* into Jesus' likeness.

## Son of God

We have an Australian Shepherd/ Border collie blue merle named Togo. He was named Togo after the great Siberian husky who famously saved the lives of children by heroically braving a blizzard in Alaska in 1925. However, our Togo turned out to be the exact opposite. He's a giant chicken.

He may be a chicken, but if there's one thing I can say about our dog, he knows who loves him. Last year, we had my parents watch our dog when we went to Ecuador for three weeks. Upon our return, we went to get him from my parents. When we came to the door, he was very happy to see us but refused to come with us.

Lying on the floor, he did not allow us to put his leash on. Suddenly, he ran backwards towards my mom, who was sitting in her La-Z-Boy, and jumped directly onto her lap.

Satisfied and resolute, he lay there with a silly grin, panting happily. He had found the one who loved him, and he didn't want to leave. Love compelled him to remain in the place he had experienced love.

Just as Togo found his place of safety in a lap, the disciple John found his identity in a posture of closeness. The book of John was written by John the Beloved, a disciple of Jesus. This disciple is the only one who referred to himself as the "one whom Jesus loved" (John 13:23). Jesus loved them all, but John is the only one who really embraced it such that it became his identity. He was the one who leaned on Jesus' chest, and I believe he never left that posture in his heart.

He was the only disciple found present at the crucifixion, and he was the first to see the empty tomb of the risen Christ. John's relationship with Jesus was singularly intimate, as he was the only one who lay on Jesus's chest. *This* is the man that God chose to be able to write arguably the most intimate words that Jesus ever spoke, because his perspective of Jesus's heart was unique. John the Beloved penned the words of prayer that Jesus spoke to the Father just before His crucifixion. This account is *only* found in John 17.

John 17 is the most intimate gaze we have of Jesus' prayer life. It is often referred to as the "High Priestly Prayer," and it is a profound, revealing chapter where Jesus, the Son prays to God, the Father through God, the Holy Spirit. It is an inside look at the fellowship of pure love in oneness and abiding. This is the only place in scripture that we see the trinity on display in such a glorious manner.

## That They Might Be One

Although it's important to consider Jesus' prayer for Himself and for the disciples, we are going to focus on the last section of His prayer: where Jesus prays for all believers. It's a short seven verses, but within those seven verses, a world of exploration awaits us.

Jesus prayed, *"I do not pray for these (disciples) alone, but also for those who will believe in Me through their word; that they all may be one, as You, Father, are in Me, and I in You; that they also may be one in Us, that the world may believe that You sent Me. And the glory which You gave Me I have given them, that they may be one just as We are one: I am in them, and You in Me; that they may be made perfect in one, and that the world may know that You have sent Me, and have loved them as You have loved Me.*

*"Father, I desire that they also whom You gave Me may be with Me where I am, that they may behold My glory which You have given Me; for You loved Me before the foundation of the world. O righteous Father! The world has not known You, but I have known You; and these have known that You sent Me. And I have declared to them Your name, and will declare it, that the love with which You loved Me may be in them, and I in them."*

To begin our exploration into Jesus' prayer, we are going to start with the first desire He listed: that they would be *one*.

The word "one" is the word "heis" in Greek. It means abundantly one another, or another of the same. Oneness is a fusion of two things coming together that are unique, but of the same kind. In the same way that the Father, Son and

Holy Spirit are completely unique, but *wholly one* in their desires.

Jesus didn't just pray that all believers would be "one" in the sense that they could all be unified- His prayer was much deeper than that. His prayer was that we would be one *just as* the Father, Son and Spirit are one. Meaning, that all believers would have *the same heart* that God Himself has for us.

In praying for all believers, Jesus uses the word "loved" three times. If His emphasis was on love, let's look a little deeper. The words "God is" are only used four times in scripture. One of them is that God *is love*. (1 John 4:8). Love is who God is- He cannot "be" without being love. What is love? Love is the Greek word, *agapao*. Some have described the word's spirit as broken down into two different Greek root words: ago, which means to lead as a shepherd leads his sheep, and pao, which means rest. Picture Psalm 23 here!

God's shepherding love brings us to a love-banquet of affection, benevolence, being plentifully fed, and well rested. Here, we're never alone, and our cups run over! Keep in mind that a shepherd does not just have one sheep- we are with a flock. The love experience with God is being perfectly led into the same peace and abundance that those around us following Jesus can also experience.

Love is other-centered, self-giving, and it always must have a partner, because you cannot love by yourself. *Love must be done between two or more parties to be defined as love.*

Love always involves a community- it is never isolated. Because of this, *you cannot have self- love.*

---

*Love must be done between two or more parties to be defined as love.*

---

Our culture today is inundated with materials on self-love. Magazines, social media and beauty products all scream for our attention to pamper ourselves and feel our own emotions. Influencers demand that there are more than two genders, there must be "safe rooms" and there is a complete lack of self-denial. Today's culture thrives on these as almost a new kind of religion. I know of people who simply do not show up to work because they don't "feel like going." This self-centered life is a broken cistern- there is never any life outside of union with others.

You only truly love when you receive love from God and give love to another. This is what we see beautifully displayed in the Father, Son, and Holy Spirit. Love loving love unto more love.

In fact, the Godhead loved so much that that love spilled over. What do you do when you can't contain the love you have for your spouse anymore? You come together as one, and a child is created from that love. That child looks like you- it is a multiplication of your image. This is exactly what God did when love spilled over. They (the Godhead) made more of themselves in humanity.

Genealogies can be long and boring, but I specifically love and appreciate the genealogy at the beginning of Luke. Luke 3:23 begins a long line of people, starting with Jesus coming as the son of Joseph, the son of Heli... and so forth for about 14 verses. I usually skip to the end of these long genealogies and my eyes gloss over, but something at the end of Luke caught my eye.

The genealogy ends with Luke 3:38. It says, "... the son of Enosh, the son of Seth, the son of Adam, the son of God." Did you catch it? Adam is listed as a *son of God* in a historical genealogy!

---

*Adam is listed as a son of God!*

---

To fully embrace the truth that we have been called to love as God loves, you must understand that *we are* "of" God. If we are not born of God, how can we ever be like Him? Adam truly was a son of God. Why, being descendants of Adam, do we have a hard time see ourselves as being born "of" God? John, the beloved knew that we were. He wrote many verses about this truth:

- **John 1:12-13**: " *But as many as received Him, to them He gave the right to become children of God,* *to those who believe in His name. Children born not of natural descent, nor of human decision or a husband's will, but born of God."*

- **1 John 3:1**: *"See what great love the Father has lavished on us, that we should be called children of God!*
- **John 3:3**: *"Jesus replied, 'Very truly I tell you, no one can see the kingdom of God unless they are born again.'"*
- **John 3:5**: *"Jesus answered, 'Very truly I tell you, no one can enter the kingdom of God unless they are born of water and the Spirit.'"*
- **1 John 3:9**: *"No one who is born of God will continue to sin, because God's seed remains in them; they cannot go on sinning, because they have been born of God."*
- **1 John 4:7**: *"Dear friends, let us love one another, for love comes from God. Everyone who loves has been born of God and knows God."*
- **1 John 5:1**: "*Everyone who believes that Jesus is the Christ is born of God, and everyone who loves the father loves his child as well."*
- **1 John 5:4**: *"For everyone born of God overcomes the world. This is the victory that has overcome the world, even our faith."*
- **1 John 5:18**: *"We know that anyone born of God does not continue to sin; the One who was born of*

*God keeps them safe, and the evil one cannot harm them."*

If we are truly the offspring of God, it should come as no surprise that because God is one, we also can be one, because we are all born of Him. This is why when Jesus prayed, "...that they all may be one, as You, Father, *are* in Me, and I in You; *that they also may be one in Us..."* (John 17:21, author's emphasis).

What does it mean to be "one"? It means that within your unique framework and design, you find agreement with one truth: Jesus. He is the way, the truth and the life. John 14:6 reads, ""I am the way and the truth and the life. No one comes to the Father except through me." If Father, Son, and Holy Spirit are one, and we only get to the Father thru Jesus, we must see Him as *the way* to oneness. There is no other path that will produce the same results. Being one in no way diminishes your unique individuality. In fact, it many ways, it enhances your individuality to celebrate God as our creator. God has so many facets to who He is, and each of us are an aspect of His likeness.

Another way I can explain what this oneness looks like is the four living creatures in the book of Revelation (Rev. 4:6-8). The four creatures are distinctly different. One is like a lion, one like an ox, one with a face like a man, and the last one is like a flying eagle. However, they are all singularly occupied with looking at one object: the man on the throne. *They have come into agreement with who they center upon and therefore have oneness in their vision.* Oneness is not uniformity, but a celebration of diversity.

---

*Oneness is not uniformity, but a celebration of diversity.*

---

We need this oneness because of how differently we are created. We all have varying giftings, talents, desires and motivations- but we should have a single focus that our lives revolve around.

God is not expecting us to figure out this whole love and oneness thing by ourselves, but to find our oneness *in Him*. Our oneness will come from humanity discovering that we are of Him, and in Him. We are *inside* the "Us" of God Himself! When that revelation truly strikes your heart, you will be empowered to experience this oneness.

Why is that oneness important? Jesus reveals one reason why at the end of the first part of His prayer: "... that the world may believe that You sent Me."

One of the greatest evangelistic strategies we have come from Jesus. When Christians love one another, they display God's likeness in the Earth. John 13:35 says, "*By this all will know that you are My disciples, if you have love for one another.*" Upon seeing such countercultural phenomenon as oneness, the world will believe that the Father sent the Son.

## The Father's Accepting Embrace

The first time my husband held our little baby girl in his arms, all he could do was smile. His face near hers, he leaned and gently kissed her rosy, red cheeks a thousand times. His arms completely encompassed her, enveloping her in safety and acceptance. He would sit and rock her, staring at the wonder of the new creation in his arms. Her beauty was enough to arrest his heart. The smile on his face stayed for days, and as he introduced grandma, grandpa and friends, he would beam with pride. His iPhone was suddenly packed with detailed photos of every furrowed eyebrow, movement of her mouth, or stretch of her arms. Our baby girl was perfect in every way, completely accepted.

God gave us the gift of family so that we could experience the Kingdom in a very real way in the Earth. How Ramiro saw our newborn daughter in the truest sense conveys Abba's feelings about us. The revelation of the Father's heart towards us as His children is one of the primary revelations that Jesus came to show us in the new covenant.

It is also the one of the primary reasons the Pharisees wanted to kill Him.

There are three times in scripture before the crucifixion that the Pharisees tried to kill Jesus. Two of times, the rage was unleased simply because Jesus identified Himself as the "Son of God." The first time, in John 5, Jesus had just healed the paralytic by the pool of Bethesda. After the healing, Jesus declared that "the Father was working with Him" to perform the miracle. John 5:17-18 says, "The Jews sought all the more to kill Him, because He not only broke the Sabbath, but also said that God was His Father, *making Himself equal* with God."

The Pharisees came to kill Jesus a second time later in John 10:22-39- this time they came with stones. The reason? Jesus was teaching people in the temple, "I and My Father are one." Once again, Jesus had proclaimed His deity by declaring that His Sonship meant oneness with the Father.

Infuriated, the Pharisees reach for their murder weapons. Instead of running away, or meeting violence with violence, Jesus simply asks them why they want to kill Him. They replied, *"For a good work we do not stone You, but for blasphemy, and because You, being a Man, make Yourself God."* They accused Jesus of *making Himself.* Now, you must slow down, stop and imagine this moment. This is a World Wrestling Entertainment (WWE) faceoff in the spirit realm if we could pull back the curtains! The religious spirit is about to have a showdown with the Holy Spirit:

Jesus responds by saying, *"Is it not written in your law, 'I said, you are gods?'"*

Ladies and gentlemen, this is a mic drop moment. The tension in the atmosphere must have been palpable. Jesus is quoting from the Law, and all religious leaders at that time were required to have had it memorized. As soon as He mentions Psalm 82, they know exactly what the words are. In Psalm 82, God is speaking to His people. God says, "I (God) said, "You *are* gods, and all of you *are* children of the Most High." (NKJV).

Jesus pointed out that *in their own law* (the one they were accusing Jesus of violating), the Word says they *all* were gods- they *all* are children of the Most High. He was saying, "not only am I the Son of God, but the law you so zealously uphold teaches that *you are* as well."

Now, most translations have the word "gods" with a lowercase "g." However, in both Greek and Hebrew languages that the Old and New Testament were translated from, they do not have capital letters. The original translation would have been neither lowercase nor uppercase. For centuries, the church has taught that we are lesser gods, but that simply is not the case, and Jesus cleared that up.

We are not 'gods' apart from Him, but we are 'of His kind'—just as a drop of ocean water is exactly the same substance as the ocean itself. This reveals our staggering identity: we are created to be bearers of the Divine Nature. As 2 Peter 1:4 echoes, we have been invited into a union so deep that we share in His very life, carrying His authority as sons and daughters of the Most High.

---

*The religious spirit hates the revelation of Abba.*

---

Both times that Jesus claims to be the Son of God, the Pharisees were so vehemently angry, they tried to kill Him. The religious spirit *hates* the revelation of Abba. Why would this single revelation make them so mad?

Someone with a legalistic, religious spirit does not think about the next generation, or training and raising spiritual children to have greater success than their own. The Pharisees primarily desired the praise of men, and wanted people to see their outward religious behavior, but had no real intention of loving those around them. John 12:43 says, *"For they loved the praise of men more than the praise of God."* A person with a Pharisee heart only wants to instruct others but does not want to raise sons and daughters to step on their shoulders.

The Pharisees were experts in the law, but the law had no desire for mercy. Their desire for judgement and the law partnered to bring about death. James 1:15 speaks about these negative desires. It says, "Then, when desire has conceived, it gives birth to sin; and sin, when it is full-grown, brings forth death."

The murderous spirit partners with the religious spirit to stop the revelation of belonging in the Father from ever being known!

The Pharisees' "weapon" was the Tree of the Knowledge of Good and Evil. They used "The Law" to try to kill "The Life."

---

*The murderous spirit partners with the religious spirit to stop the revelation of belonging in the Father from ever being known!*

---

Have you ever experienced suicidal thoughts, or feelings of self-hate, or self-harm? This is the root system of those thoughts. They all stem from a lie: that you are an unacceptable orphan.

If this lie can produce death with such power and force, what would happen if we believed the opposite: that we were born perfectly acceptable into His family? Can you fathom the degree of the power of life we would walk in if we really believed that right now, we are His, and He's crazy about us and thinks we are outrageously desirable?

Psalm 103:13 reads, *"As a father pities his children, so the LORD pities those who fear Him."* The word "pities" that is used there is a weak translation. The real word is "racham," and it means to love or mercy, especially by compassion. This word is specifically used regarding how parents love their infant child.

In fact, the Hebrew word for "womb" is "racham."

A better way to read that verse with the translation in mind is to think about a father, looking at their perfect, newborn baby- like my husband, or any husband does with their child. From the womb, that baby has not sinned, is perfectly whole, and completely innocent. Having done absolutely nothing in his life to *earn* his inheritance or provision, the father freely and generously provides a home, food, and shelter. He does this not by compulsion, manipulation, regret or anger, but because of deeply rooted love and acceptance. He does it simply because the baby is His child.

You are that child.

# CHAPTER SIX

# It Is to Your Advantage

The leader who pastored me in the early years of my salvation passed away very suddenly. In the ensuing weeks and months after his departure, I often thought, "How are we going to make it without him?" During national tragedies or significant events, he played a crucial role in educating and equipping members of the Christian community to view these occurrences from a Biblical perspective.

A few months after his passing, hurricane Harvey hit Houston. I remember aching to be able to hear what pastor would say about the event- wishing that he could still be here with us to shepherd our hearts once again. It was the closest thing I've experienced to what the disciples must have felt like when Jesus told them that He was about to leave them.

Imaging having three years living with Jesus. You would get to wake up with Him, walk with Him, ask Him questions whenever you wanted. If something crazy was going on, you'd look to Him for leadership, wisdom and guidance. You'd get to be brave and walk out on waters, knowing He'd catch you if you sunk. You'd get to see crazy miracles every day and live in perfect friendship and fellowship.

Now imagine Jesus telling you that it would be better if He wasn't walking with you anymore, but that you would be better off without Him present.

What?! How in the world could life be any better than God physically walking with His disciples every day? Jesus knew of a better way to Shepherd His people than what His people could perceive. He said, *"Nevertheless I tell you the truth. It is to your advantage that I go away; for if I do not go away, the Helper will not come to you; but if I depart, I will send Him to you."*

Wait a minute... its "to our advantage" that Jesus goes away!?!

If I were a disciple that was walking with Jesus every day, I would find it very hard to believe that Him going anywhere else could possibly be *to my advantage*. Jesus was the best thing that ever happened to any of these people! I can imagine the confusion, uncertainty and disillusionment they all experienced when Jesus was crucified, the elation that He was with them again, and then the shock that He departed again.

If Jesus thought that it was to our advantage that He go away, we need to lean in and learn why. Jesus said that it would be better for us to have the Holy Spirit than it would be to have Jesus walking on the earth. That may seem confusing, but we must trust that Jesus knows what He's talking about.

Jesus knew something that the disciples didn't know- He wasn't leaving them alone as orphans. He said in John 14:16-18, *"And I will pray the Father, and He will give you another Helper, that He may abide with you forever— the Spirit of truth, whom the world cannot receive, because it neither sees Him nor knows Him; but you know Him, for He dwells with you and will be in you. I will not leave you orphans; I will come to you. A little while longer and the world will see Me no more, but you will see Me. Because I live, you will live also. At that day you will know that I am in My Father, and you in Me, and I in you."*

Far from leaving them orphans- the leaving of Jesus and the coming of the Holy Spirit were an announcement of *our joint inclusion* in the family of God! Once the Holy Spirit came, we would know by experience that Jesus is in the Father, we are in Him, and He is in us. The whole family is now together again, because of the indwelling of the power of the Holy Spirit.

How are we together? We are *in one another*. You don't get any closer than that. "In one another" means that there cannot exist division in the body.

If you are in Jesus, and I am in Jesus, and He is in the Father, and the Holy Spirit is in us- then *we are one*. The Holy Spirit is what made *this kind* of unity possible. The kind of unity where we are all distinctly different but have one singular desire that fuels us: love. I believe that this is the unity that Jesus was after in John 17 when He prayed "... that they all may be one, as You, Father, are in Me, and I in You; that they also may be one in Us, that the world may believe that You sent Me" (John 17:21).

Being "one" is one thing. Being one *just as* The Father, Son and Holy Spirit are one is something entirely different.

Jesus is a man who can only be in one place at one time- He couldn't possibly always be with every person. However, the Holy Spirit is the constantly with us, never leaving us, always abiding forever union of God *within*! In fact, John 14:16 says, "...He (the Holy Spirit) may abide with you forever." Forever? Yes, forever! The word forever is the Greek word "aion," which signifies *eternal existence*. Introduce yourself to your forever and ever roommate!

And this is the advantage Jesus was talking about. Not a consolation prize for losing Him — but an upgrade into something that couldn't have happened any other way. Jesus, as a man, could only be in one place. He could walk beside you, but He couldn't live *inside* you. The Holy Spirit doesn't just visit — He takes up permanent residence. That's not a lesser arrangement. *That's the whole point.* The indwelling power of the Holy Spirit on the inside of each believer is what the Father, Son and Spirit had in mind all along!

Your new "Roommate" doesn't just share your space; He shares your identity. He is the one who constantly reminds us of the "Born of God" DNA we discussed in the last chapter.

40 days after the crucifixion of Jesus, Jesus' disciples began to pray in Jerusalem. They were following Jesus' last words, “Behold, I send the Promise of My Father upon you; but tarry in the city of Jerusalem until you are endued with power from on high" (Luke 24:49). I can imagine what the next few days were like. Jesus said many confusing things that the disciples often had a hard time understanding.

Now He just wants them to wait in Jerusalem? For an extended period? I wonder how many of His disciples started the prayer meeting but did not see it through to the end.

Oneness isn't just a feeling we fall into; it's often the fruit of staying in the room together until the 'Promise' arrives.

Ten days after Jesus' ascension, 120 were still praying together in an upper room on the day of Pentecost, a Jewish feast. Can you guess how the book of Acts describes the ten days that they were praying? In unity!! With *one* accord. "These all continued with one accord in prayer, and supplication, with the women and Mary the mother of Jesus, and with His brothers." (Acts 1:14). The phrase "one accord" is a word that means "unanimously- with one mind."

When we do what Jesus asks us to do, *unity is produced.*

As they prayed in unity, the moment they had been waiting for came. *"Suddenly, there came a sound from heaven, as of a rushing mighty wind, and it filled the whole house where they were sitting"* (Acts 2:2).

What did it sound like when Holy Spirit came? Do you think they experienced the building shaking, or could they hear a train approaching- like a tornado? Maybe the wind whipped around like a hurricane. I've been in all of those, and they're scary! Nothing like this has ever happened before in all human history! Imagine waking up on a normal day at nine AM... doing your chores, walking to the market, or heading back from the fishing boat only to look up and hear a spot where a single building was filled with rushing wind!

The people individually heard a sound and saw the fire- but what happened next was profound. When Holy Spirit came, the *sound* of His coming *caused even more people to gather*. *"And when this sound occurred, the multitude came together, and were confused, because everyone heard them speak in his own language"* (Acts 2:6, author's emphasis).

A small group in unity results in multitudes being gathered to join the unity that exists.

The sound of Holy Spirit brought a new sound out of God's people: they spoke with tongues. That sound was not divisive, but the sound *drew the unbelievers*.

The gift of the Holy Spirit on the Day of Pentecost was not just a singular event, but God's invitation to empowering unity that extends to all believers. As we embrace this gift, we recognize that we are not left as orphans but are brought into an intimate relationship with God, united by His Spirit. This unity transcends languages and cultural barriers, creating a community that reflects the heart and love of the Father. Far from being a gift that caused division, tongues ushered in salvation, unity, and unprecedented church growth.

# CHAPTER SEVEN

## Unifying Languages

As I sat in the giant massage chair for my pedicure, Vietnamese could be heard nonstop from the workers in the nail salon. Across from me were two older ladies who were Spanish, and my mom and I who spoke English. One of the ladies who was working on my pedicure asked me a question that I couldn't understand- even though she was using an English word. Her thick accent made it impossible for me to pick out the word she was trying to use. I asked her to repeat it, but I still didn't understand.

Frustrated, I turned to my mom to ask her if she could figure it out, and the Vietnamese woman painting my toes asked her co-worker. None of us could figure it out, so we all shrugged at one another, smiled and laughed. The two ladies speaking Spanish paused, and seeing they couldn't help, continued speaking to one another. Their fast Spanish was a background to the language dog-pile.

The six of us struggled to communicate. The language barrier was frustrating, but comical as we all gave up, laughing and smiling. We understood that we couldn't do anything to bridge the gap and express ourselves the way we wanted to. The separation of languages was an invisible wall.

Language is fundamental to being understood. It's virtually impossible to communicate well without speaking the same language. Without some kind of unification in language, unity in heart is all but impossible.

Of all languages, there is one language that has been the most confusing: tongues. There has been a lot of turmoil over tongues in denominational Christianity. It seems to be a divisive gift, but I believe the exact opposite is true. I believe that the gift of tongues is the most *unifying gift* that God ever gave the church, because that's what we see displayed the first time the gift is ever used.

The Law of First Mention is a principle used in biblical interpretation. According to this principle, the first time a word, concept, or doctrine appears in the Bible provides the foundational meaning and context for understanding that word, concept, or doctrine throughout the rest of Scripture. The first time a concept appears in scripture, it holds a foundational truth that sets a precedent for all other related activity.

The first time that we saw tongues in scripture, all 120 praying saints received the language, and the language *attracted* unbelievers. It was a unifying event, where the gospel was preached, and salvations occurred.

*"When the Day of Pentecost had fully come, they were all with one accord in one place. And suddenly there came a sound from heaven, as of a rushing mighty wind, and it filled the whole house where they were sitting. Then there appeared to them divided tongues, as of fire, and one sat upon each of them. And they were all filled with the Holy Spirit and began to speak with other tongues, as the Spirit gave them utterance"* (Acts 2:1-4).

Some churches teach that tongues are only a spontaneous utterance of other languages so that people will hear you declaring God. They believe it's for missionaries in foreign places who are suddenly filled with understanding of a new language. Although this can happen, it's not the most used form of tongues.

One of my mentors used to work at a house of prayer years ago. One time, he told a story of an event that happened in the prayer room. Their prayer room is 24/7, and they have had constant praise, worship and thanksgiving with songs and prayers for over 25 years. Anyone can come in and out of the prayer room, day or night, to sit in the presence of God. One evening, a woman was up at the front singing in tongues, while the band played, and others sang. In the back of the room, and Native American man quietly snuck in and sat down. Suddenly, the man burst into tears and ran to the front saying, "How do you know that language?"

The woman was singing in her normal devotional tongue that she had prayed with for years. But the man, who was from a native American tribe, still spoke the language of his ancestors- one that was almost extinct. In fact, there were only at the time a handful of people that knew this language. Sobbing he said, "You keep saying over and over "I love you and hold you like a mother holds their baby." His heart was won to the Lord that day, and he was marvelously saved.

I'm convinced that on the day of Pentecost, when the church was baptized by the Holy Spirit with fire, it was just like this testimony I heard. I believe that all the 120 received their tongue, and that in receiving their tongue, it opened the ears of the unbelievers around them to hear in their native language.

The power of this one language cannot be underestimated.

In fact, when Paul wrote to the Corinthian church, he emphasized that their speech would have a lot to do with their unity. He wrote, *"Now I plead with you, brethren, by the name of our Lord Jesus Christ, that you all speak the same thing, and that there be no divisions among you, but that you be perfectly joined together in the same mind and in the same judgement"* (1 Cor. 1:10).

Having one language is not unprecedented in human history. There was a point in history where all the people on the earth had one language. Gen 11:1 says, *"Now the whole earth had one language and one speech."* At the time when the earth only had one language, the people came together in a *unity* that has not been witnessed on the earth since that time. It is important to note that there was, at one time, a unity on earth- but it wasn't godly.

The people with one language said, "Come, let us build for ourselves a city... lest *we be scattered* abroad over the efface of the whole earth." (Gen. 11:4, author's emphasis). The earliest people understood the need for unity to avoid being scattered. What is fascinating, however, is God's response to the people's evil attempts to make their name great:

"*But the LORD came down to see the city and the tower which the sons of men had built. And the LORD said, "Indeed the people are one and they all have one language, and this is what they begin to do; now nothing that they propose to do will be withheld from them" (Gen 11:5-6).*

With one language, nothing will be impossible for the people.

Because God knew the power of one language, and He did not want His people to build something demonic, He came down and confused the people's language. Remember how we talked about how having one language unifies the people? When God confused the languages of the people on earth, they *scattered*. Gen. 11:9 says, *"... the LORD confused the language of all the earth; and from there the LORD scattered them abroad over the face of all the earth."*

With divided language, *the people scatter*.

That's not the end of the story, however. Thousands of years later, an Old Testament prophet named Zephaniah comes on the scene. Zephaniah's name means "The LORD has hidden," and I think God did indeed hide something in his prophetic words for us to find. The book of Zephaniah speaks of God's mercy and faithful ability to restore His people. In Zephaniah 3:8, God begins to describe a day of redemption in the future when everything would change:

*"Therefore, wait for Me," says the LORD, "Until the day I rise up for plunder; My determination is to gather the nations to My assembly of kingdoms, to pour on them My indignation, all my fierce anger; all the earth shall be devoured with the fire of My jealousy."*

Can you see the events of the book of Acts playing out in this verse? First, the disciples *waited* in the upper room- just like the beginning of the verse describes when God instructs them to wait for Him. Then, God says He will *gather all the nations*- just like all the nations were gathered at the feast of Pentecost. Finally, God describes the *fire of His jealousy* devouring the earth- just like the tongues of fire that appeared on the disciple's heads.

God's fire came not to destroy His people, but to destroy everything that hindered the unity of love. This is what the baptism of the Holy Spirit and fire always intended to do!

I heard a story of a woman that had deadly cancer. The lymphoma was so bad, her doctors said that it was the worst case they had ever seen. She was on a ventilator, getting ready to die. While on her deathbed, a pastor came to the hospital to pray for her. As the pastor sat at the edge of the bed, all he could think about was how much he wanted to crawl inside every cell of her body that was killing her and destroy them. He was furious at the disease that was taking her life. Suddenly, Holy Spirit spoke to his heart and said, "*That's my wrath. I came to destroy everything that stops fullness of life in my people.*"

That fire that came into the upper room at Pentecost was to destroy the scattering, disunity that had been corrupting God's desire for unity for generations. What happens after this fire falls?

Zephaniah 3:9 says, "*For then I will restore to the peoples a pure language, that they all may call on the name of the LORD, to serve Him with one accord.*"

Pentecost was the undoing of the division at the tower of Babel. We now have one language restored, and according to scripture, this means that nothing will be impossible for us. Instead of being scattered, we can now be gathered under the leadership of the Holy Spirit. God made a way for His people to be one *just as* He is one.

## No Longer Scattered

Holy Spirit's leadership continuously dominates the storyline in the book of Acts. The Book of Acts, also known as the Acts of the Apostles, is sometimes informally referred to as the Acts of the Holy Spirit due to the prominent role that the Holy Spirit plays throughout the narrative. In the first 8 chapters alone, the Holy Spirit is mentioned 24 times!

After the arrival of Holy Spirit as the leader of God's people, the church enjoyed a time of incredible growth, with multitudes being added to their number daily. But the great move of Holy Spirit with signs, miracles, wonders and salvation wasn't just all without pushback- the move of God stirred up intense persecution. A pharisee named Saul, a devout Hellenistic Jew from the tribe of Benjamin, was determined to round up every one of these new believers and arrest them. Saul had the highest religious education that was possible in that day, and *this* was the man who was the most actively involved in persecuting early Christians.

As the persecution increased, the Christians *scattered.* *"Now Saul was consenting to his (Stephen the Martyr's) death. At that time a great persecution arose against the church which was at Jerusalem; and they were all scattered throughout the regions of Judea and Samaria, except the apostles"* (Acts 8:1-4).

But remember, the Holy Spirit is now the new leader of the Church. Every single believer always has access to the leadership and empowerment of God Himself.

Under this new leadership of the Holy Spirit, that scattering was no longer a scattering because of a lost leader. Because each believer was now empowered with Holy Spirit, the scattering caused *the gospel to be preached everywhere*! Acts 8:4 says, "*Therefore those who were scattered went everywhere preaching the word. Then Philip when down to the city of Samaria and preached Christ to them. And the multitudes with one accord heeded the things spoken by Philip, hearing and seeing the miracles which he did*" (Acts 8:4-6).

Because the believers now each personally had a live-in leader in Holy Spirit, the scattering became a blessing. In fact, the scattering brought *multitudes* into the "one accord" that they had obtained with the infilling of the Holy Spirit.

*Once again, Holy Spirit brought unity.*

As they went from city to city, they laid hands on others, and they also received the Holy Spirit. This was such a dramatic change and encounter, a sorcerer wanted to be able to have the power he saw displayed! These people were seeing unclean spirits leave, the lame and paralyzed healed, and experiencing great joy! Under the leadership of Holy Spirit, the church prospered greatly in the persecution.

The book of Acts is a picture of what the church, filled with the Holy Spirit, can do. Thousands were being saved, healed, delivered, and these apostolic leaders literally turned the world upside down (Acts 17:6). Not one time is anyone ever asked to repeat a prayer to go to heaven, but the kingdom of God was displayed. The works that Jesus did were done by His apostles, and even *greater* miracles. The

Holy Spirit's infilling fueled these early Christians to spread the gospel with boldness, authority, and fearlessness.

## More Unity

As the church spread, and the gospel was preached to cities near and far, the apostle Peter stopped on his missionary journey at housetop to pray. (Acts 10:9). He fell into a trance and saw an open vision of a great sheet with four corners. In the sheet were all kinds of animals. Acts 10:19 says, "*While Peter thought about this vision, the Spirit said to him, "Behold, three men are seeking you. Arise therefore, go down and go with them, doubting nothing; for I have sent them."*

Following the Holy Spirit's leadership, Peter follows the men to Cornelius's house. Cornelius was a devout man who prayed and fasted often but was not Jewish. Until this time, the Jewish people did not think that Gentiles were part of their covenant with God. According to the law, Peter was not allowed to eat or fellowship with these people!

But under the leadership of the Holy Spirit, Peter began to preach to Cornelius's whole household the good news of Jesus- who was anointed with the Holy Spirit and power to do good and heal all who were oppressed by the devil (Acts 1-:34-43). As Peter preached the gospel to the unbelievers in the household, the Holy Spirit fell upon all those who heard him preach. *"And those of the circumcision who believed were astonished, as many as came with Peter, because the gift of the Holy Spirit had been poured out on the Gentiles also. For they heard them speak with tongues and magnify God."* (Acts 10:44-46).

You need to understand how big a deal this was. They were *astonished*. This would have been a jaw dropping, mind blowing, history shaking event! Since the beginning of Abraham's journey with God, only *one* people group had been chosen to represent God in the earth: the Jewish people. They were set apart, and Holy unto the Lord, different from every other people group.

For just over two thousand years, the Jewish nation alone was able to call God *their God*. The Torah, the Jewish scriptures, had laws to keep the Israeli people away from Gentiles to prevent the Jews from adopting idolatrous behaviors. These laws included restrictions on social interactions, dietary laws, and many others.

But Holy Spirit's leadership was about to change those two thousand years of division in a single moment.

In one baptism of the Holy Spirit, God bridged the gap of division, and Holy Spirit welcomed the Gentiles into a grafted-in union under one God. The preaching of the gospel and the manifestation of the Holy Spirit brought an unprecedented unity to the earth.

If Babel was the wall between nations, and the Law was the wall between Jew and Gentile, then the Holy Spirit was the wrecking ball that leveled them both.

Once again, the gift of tongues was present when God announced the inclusion of the Gentile people into the Jewish covenant. The same Holy Spirit that had been poured out at Pentecost was now poured out in the same measure upon this Gentile household. The Holy Spirit, with one language, brought all people groups of the earth together into one covenant.

Jesus' prayer was closer than ever to being answered.

# CHAPTER EIGHT

# Decline and Rise of the Spirit

Around 100-150 years after Jesus' ascension, the church, which had been multiplying and growing, began a drastic decline. Internal conflicts began to rage between people groups. The Roman authorities began severe persecution, and heresies began to emerge. Over time, Buddhism, Hinduism, Islam, Sikh, Scientology and other religions developed. For centuries, Holy Spirit took a back seat to religious scholars and man-made religion.

When the Church loses its "Oneness," it loses its ability to represent the True Light, allowing other "isms" to fill the void.

However, if you look back through history, you will find years and seasons where there was great revival that looked and sounded like the early church in Acts. *Every single time revival broke out*, you will find that the Holy Spirit was at the very center. Here is a short list of revivals that took place:

**Clairvaux Abbey (12th Century):**

In the Middle Ages, under the influence of St. Bernard of Clairvaux, Clairvaux Abbey became a center of spiritual renewal and reform. The monks at Clairvaux Abbey engaged in continuous prayer and contemplation, seeking to be filled with the Holy Spirit and to live a life of holiness. St. Bernard, a monk, established the abbey with a group of twelve other monks. This abbey birthed 250 monasteries across Europe, establishing praying people in many places.

**Martin Luther (1510):**

On July 2, 1510, Luther had a profound experience while studying Romans 1:17, which states, "The just shall live by faith." He felt as though the gates of paradise had opened, and he experienced a deep sense of assurance and peace.

This encounter with the Holy Spirit led Luther to understand that salvation is a gift of God's grace received through faith, not by works. This revelation was completely counter-cultural and turned the religious world upside down. His encounter with the Holy Spirit sparked the Protestant Reformation, challenging the practices and doctrines of the Catholic Church. Luther's experience with the Holy Spirit revealing biblical truths rocked the structure of the entire church.

**Pietistic Revival (1675):**

A revival broke out on the continent of Europe in Germany known as the Pietistic Revival. Beginning in 1675, its leaders were Philip Spener, a theologian and professor, and August Franke. Their emphasis was on justification that Luther had emphasized two centuries earlier at the outbreak of the Protestant Reformation. They gave special attention to sanctification, emphasizing not just believing correct doctrine but also experiencing the Holy Spirit. There was a strong emphasis on the power of prayer and being filled with the Holy Spirit.

**The Moravians (1727):**

The Moravians, also known as the Moravian Brethren, are one of the oldest Protestant denominations, dating back to the 15th century. Their revival, often referred to as the Great Moravian Revival, took place in 1727 at the estate of Count Nicholas Ludwig Zinzendorf in Herrnhut, Germany. The community at Herrnhut experienced a powerful outpouring of the Holy Spirit. Historians describe it as a day when the Holy Spirit came upon them with great signs and wonders. The Moravians sustained day and night worship and prayer 24/7 at their settlement in Germany for over 100 years. From this day and night place of devotion to Jesus, missionary pioneers were sent out all over the world.

**Methodist Revival (1730's and 40's):**

John Wesley was the leader of this historic movement. Wesley experienced his conversion at a Moravian meeting on Aldersgate Street. He was filled with the Holy Spirit around 3 a.m. during an observance meeting of the Lord's Supper on Fetter's Lane. John Wesley experienced a profound spiritual awakening. This event marked a turning point in his ministry and life. Wesley emphasized the importance of prayer, worship, and the experience of the Holy Spirit. This move of the Holy Spirit started the Wesleyan church, a church that today has over 1 million members.

**The Great Awakening (1730s and 1740):**

George Whitfield was a key figure in the Great Awakening, which was a series of religious revivals in the British American colonies during the 18th century. Although he had many, his first significant encounter with the Holy Spirit occurred during his time at Oxford University. While he was a student, Whitefield experienced a profound spiritual awakening. This revival was not called the Great Awakening when it was occurring, but rather the Great Clamor or Noise because of the activity of the Holy Spirit. Scores of thousands came to the Lord at a time when the population of the colonies was about two million.

**The Second Great Awakening and Charles Finney (1792-1875):**

Charles Finney was a prominent American preacher and theologian who played a key role in the Second Great Awakening, a series of Christian revivals in the early 19th century. Although he was a lawyer by occupation, Finney experienced a dramatic conversion in the autumn of 1821 while working. He described it as a powerful baptism of the Holy Spirit, which he felt as a wave of liquid love and joy that seemed to go through his body and soul. He left his profession and pursued preaching of the gospel. He is often called the Father of Modern Revivalism.

**Cain Ridge Revival (1801):**

Beginning in the context of preparation for the annual Lord's Supper celebration among the Scottish Presbyterians, the people were baptized with a fresh infilling of Holy Spirit. Before long, the news of what happened went far and wide, and people came from long distances to experience the outpouring. They came by foot, horse, wagon and train. It is estimated that crowds of 20,000 came to camp out in tents and wagons for the meetings at Cane

Ridge. Manifestations of the Holy Spirit included crying, shaking, jerking, falling under His power, as well as children preaching and sharing biblical knowledge they did not have in the natural. Within one to two years from the start of this revival, one-fourth of all Christians in the south had experienced these manifestations.

**Welsh Revival (1904-1905):**

The revival began with a day of prayer and fasting called by Charles Parham and Seth Joshua on September 22, 1904. During this meeting, Evan Roberts received an infilling of the Holy Spirit. His life and ministry were deeply impacted that day by the Holy Spirit. Roberts and his friends experienced the baptism of the Holy Spirit and were marked by God's presence and power. It is remembered as one of the purest outpourings of the Holy Spirit in the history of the church.

**Azusa Street Revival (1906-1915):**

Azusa Street Revival was a historic series of revival meetings that took place in Los Angeles, California. It was led by William J. Seymour, an African American preacher. The revival began in a former African Methodist Episcopal church building at 312 Azusa Street in the industrial section of Los Angeles.

The revival began when three men started to pray. The Holy Spirit came with such power, the fire department was called because they thought the church was on fire! There was glowing flames like light that shot up into the sky. Historically, the building at 312 Azusa Street never actually caught fire or suffered fire damage during the revival. Upon the fire department's arrival, they found no physical fire, no smoke, and no heat. Instead, they found a room full of people in intense, spontaneous worship.

Azusa street had many notable manifestations of the Holy Spirit- speaking in tongues, healings, shaking, laughter and joy, prophecy, visions, and sustained worship.

**Toronto Blessing (1994-2000):**

The Toronto Blessing was a significant Christian revival that began in January 1994 at the Toronto Airport Vineyard Church. The revival was known for powerful encounters with the Holy Spirit, including laughter, shaking, and falling under the Spirit's power. The revival was led by John and Carol Arnott, who were seeking a deeper move of the Holy Spirit.

**Brownsville Revival (1995-2000):**

I personally know people who attended the revival at Brownsville in Pensacola, Florida. This revival began on Father's Day in 1995 and was sustained for five glorious years. The power of the Holy Spirit touched many during the meetings, and the line just to get in the building was hours long. My pastor attended one weekend of services, and he and his wife came back completely changed- unable to describe the experience in words.

Another set of pastors that I know went into the meeting hungry for more of God, but resistant to the gifts of the spirit. They came back from the meeting not only agreeing with the power of the gifts, but they began to teach about them in their church.

Friends I know tell me stories of what it was like just to stand in the room. The glory of God caused the atmosphere to feel electric- even outside of the building. One of my friends was hit by such a powerful move of Holy Spirit, he flew across the room and was completely delivered from oppression when he stood up- after spending hours laying on the floor under the weight of the power of the Glory of God.

There were numerous reports of supernatural healings and deliverance from various forms of bondage, including addiction and demonic oppression. People profoundly experienced God. This five-year revival had over four million people attend the revival meetings.

**Asbury Revival (2023):**

The Asbury Revival, also known as the Asbury Outpouring, began on February 8, 2023, at Asbury University in Wilmore, Kentucky. The revival started when students spontaneously stayed in Hughes Auditorium after a regularly scheduled chapel service. The atmosphere changed when a student openly confessed his sins, leading to a powerful and continuous worship session. The revival lasted for only 16 days, but there were many testimonies about the power of the Holy Spirit that was clear during the revival. It was attended by approximately 15,000 people each day.

By its end, the revival brought 50,000–70,000 visitors to Wilmore, representing more than 200 academic institutions and multiple countries.

## What's Next?

Where will the next move of God be? When will the next move of God happen? Historically, there have been great moves after periods of spiritual decline. Revivals often occur in cycles and seem to happen very unexpectedly. How can we be prepared for something that may happen at any moment? Jesus said in Matthew 24:42, "*Therefore keep watch, because you do not know on what day your Lord will come.*"

Many denominations of Christian churches that exist today were birthed out of the revivals I mentioned, or other moves of the Holy Spirit. As the church awakens to the power of the Holy Spirit once again, and we are aware of His leadership, I believe more of these revivals will begin to appear and will be sustained.

Why did these amazing moves of God stop? Historically, many revivals dispersed because of dissensions and fights among the leaders and people. *Disunity* among the people is what caused the outpouring of the Holy Spirit to cease.

## Why Does the Fire Go Out?

Historically, the pattern is consistent. Revival cools when pride creeps in and leaders begin taking credit for what the Spirit is doing. It fades when control takes over – when people try to organize and package a move of God until He is no longer free to lead.

Offense finishes the work: when "flesh and blood" conflicts distract people from the one accord they had found together. And preference seals it – when a denomination or a method becomes more important than the Person of the Spirit Himself. In every case, the fire didn't go out because God withdrew. It went out because people stopped making room for Him.

For as long as I can remember as a Christian, I have heard people speak about revival as if it's something far away, and we must do something to convince God to come and manifest Himself like this again. I prayed like that for years. However, my heart has started to shift. I do believe God will come in those amazing ways again, but I think that He's more concerned with how we're treating our spouses, children, and families and friendships.

When Jesus came and walked with humanity on the Earth, He had conversations, dinner, and interacted with people. He constantly taught about human relationships, and displayed what they should look like.

So, the question we need to answer is: how do we navigate pursuing union with one another with the leadership of the Holy Spirit? I believe one of the aspects that the church must learn to grow and understand is the very beginning of the creation of man. No, it didn't begin the moment you were born. You are eternal, and we need to explore your beginning, or your "genesis." Just like the Word began with Genesis, you began with a genesis. Before we can know who we are to one another, we must know who we are to God. From there, we can grow into a place of unity where revival can be sustained.

What is possible when just two or three come into agreement to have Holy Spirit be Lord, and lead them? Just think of it- two Apostles in personal revival "turned the world upside down" (Acts 17:6).

Maybe, just maybe, revival as we once knew it isn't what God ultimately wants after all. Maybe, He's after personal revival that leads to families being in revival that leads to churches, cities, and nations?

And maybe, that begins with us experiencing revelations from God that revolutionize our relationships and put God's power and glory on display.

## Empowered By Grace

We often revere the early church, focusing on their incredible actions. We are awed by the unity, the miracles, and the generosity of the church. But what if the true power wasn't just in what they did, but *why did they did it?*

I heard of a church that told their congregation that they needed to meet house to house every day during the week because that's what the early church did. The congregation, eager to obey so that they could witness the signs miracles and wonders of the book of Acts, quickly put host homes and small groups into action.

What do you suppose happened? They completely burnt out. No one could sustain the pace. Families were exhausted, not taken care of, and personal responsibility put to the side. People were overstretched and overtired. It was an idea found in scripture but not breathed on by the Spirit.

It is right to look to scripture for what Jesus and the apostles taught. But don't miss the tree in the forest. If you only focus on the results, you'll miss the core of what the 120 were waiting for: Holy Spirit.

The early church was only able to do what they did because the Holy Spirit came upon them and was also within them. The Church of Acts was a *product* of the indwelling of the Holy Spirit.

Acts 4:33 says, *"And with great power the apostles gave witness to the resurrection of the Lord Jesus. And great grace was upon them all."*

What if we have focused so much on the product of grace, we have forgotten about the *source* of grace? What if we've focused on giving, evangelism, teaching and gathering instead of waiting and listening for the Voice that instructed them in the first place?

Grace is God's empowerment to do the things He does. It's His ability to love, give, share and care for others. Oneness is a fruit, not a goal to be achieved by human effort.

For too long, I'm afraid we've tried to duplicate the *behaviors* of the early church, hoping for the same results, while we ignore the one who told them how to behave.

The early church experienced a profound revelation of love, grace, righteousness, and union with God because they obeyed the voice of the Jesus when He told them to "tarry in the city until they were filled with power from on high."

They didn't try to obey until they were filled with power. They didn't start meeting house to house and devoting themselves to teaching... and then be filled with the Spirit. The infilling of the Spirit happened first, and all the activities followed.

This internal shift compelled them to step outside the box of religion and do things that weren't "written." They lived from a place of radical freedom and divine leading.

This calls us to pursue internal transformation rather than mere behavior changes or routines, emphasizing guidance by the Spirit over formulas. If the Church prioritized prayer, were empowered by grace, and followed the Holy Spirit's direction, we might witness genuine signs and wonders instead of manufactured results.

---

*This calls us to pursue internal transformation rather than mere behavior changes or routines, emphasizing guidance by the Spirit over formulas.*

---

# CHAPTER NINE

# Holy Spirit's Lordship

I sat on the park bench with my heart shattered. My kids were playing on the playground, but even their loud screams and running with laughter could not make me smile. The pain, grief and rejection I was experiencing was almost more than my heart could handle. I cried for days before the Lord in prayer, with no relief in my heart or soul. One of my closest friends had betrayed me.

As I sat on that bench, the overcast sky matching my mood, my friend Ava sat next to me. I poured out my heart concerning the details of the betrayal, and Ava listened carefully to me with great compassion. We talked for over an hour, as I desperately tried to find some place of peace in my heart where I could alleviate the unrelenting, knife stabbing pain of betrayal. Suddenly, Ava looks me straight in the eyes and spoke a word of wisdom that brought a sense of peace. In a moment, I felt relief. Leaning back on the park bench, I sobbed as I said, "Thank you so much- you have no idea what those words mean to me. You are like Holy Spirit to me."

When I said, "You are like Holy Spirit to me," it felt pure. I saw her as an agent of the Holy Spirit, sent to comfort me. She cried, and I cried. After hugging one another, we both left the park. But something deeply wrong was deposited in my heart that day would not be unveiled *for years*.

Days turned into months, which turned into years that went by. One day, years later, Ava and I had a disagreement where both of us were hurt deeply. In all my years of friendship with her, we had never been in a fight, much less a fight where we were both left so wounded. It caught us both off guard and we tried as best we could to navigate reconciliation. That wounding went on for months, although both of us diligently sought the Lord for healing and reunion. We would try to get together, but both of us could feel the distance and distress from the other. We both knew the friendship was a gift from God but could not overcome the pain we both felt.

We did the only thing we knew how to do. We prayed and waited. For nine months, this wedge in our relationship continued to manifest and we *continued* to hurt one another- although the intention of both of our hearts was to bring healing.

While we were navigating this division, I began to meditate and diligently study the Lordship of the Holy Spirit out of 2 Corinthians 3. I would wake up every morning, and spend an hour or more speaking out, "Holy Spirit, you alone sit on the throne of my heart. You are Lord of my life." I did this for almost four months.

One day, Ava and I got into another disagreement. I stumbled into a trap, and felt a massive sense of self-rejection, self-hate. I walked away from our discussion feeling like I was scum of the earth and worthless. Driving home, I cried in the car desperate for some sense of clarity. The next three days turned into a nightmare of pain as thoughts tormented me. Up until this point in my life, I had never experienced anything like this level of thought warfare. It was so strong, I honestly thought that I was going through an identity crisis. There was a world of chaos inside my heart, and no amount of worship, prayer, or distraction could bring me the peace my soul craved. I was *desperate* to get out of the mess that had been made.

The morning of the third day, as I sat before the Lord, I told Him once again, "Holy Spirit, you are Lord of my life. You alone sit on the throne of my heart." Immediately, I heard the voice of God so strong, it startled me. He said, "No, I'm not. Ava is. Ava has sat as Lord on the throne of your heart for years." In disbelief, I said, "No, Lord! That's not true! Show me how that's true!" In an instant, He took me back to the park bench and I saw myself say the words, "Ava, you are like Holy Spirit to me."

I sat there, stunned. Collecting myself, I cried out, "I remove Ava from my heart! Holy Spirit, you alone are King and ruler of my life, and your opinion of me is the only one I value!"

*Immediately,* I was completely free.

I sat there for a long time. I didn't know what to do with that kind of sudden quiet inside me. It was the kind of stillness you only notice after you've been in noise for so long you forgot what silence felt like. The weight was just... gone. I hadn't realized how heavy it was until it wasn't there anymore. I laughed, and then I cried, and then I laughed again. Something had shifted in a place I hadn't even known was broken.

I mean, *it was like night and day* in an instant! I felt like I lost 100 pounds, and I could see again, breathe again, and joy began to well up inside of me. The shift was so profound, in fact, that I could say it was another type of salvation experience. The grass was greener, the sky was blue, and I felt the acceptance and love of God smother me in a way I had never received before.

Suddenly, everything began to make sense. The only reason that my close friend could reject me and cause me so much inner turmoil was because I had allowed her to be the judge of my heart. The day that my close friend betrayed me, my heart was exposed, raw and open, yearning for acceptance. My grave mistake that day was looking for and receiving affirmation and acceptance *from another person* instead of the Holy Spirit.

Don't ever give someone else the ability to determine how you feel or what you think. You alone are responsible for your own thoughts and feelings.

People will constantly disappoint and reject you, because we were only designed to have One on the throne of our hearts. If another person is allowed to have that kind of authority, all those feelings of self-hate, suicide, worthlessness and depression can overtake your life.

People are constantly rejecting thoughts or ideas throughout the day. These thoughts can range from how we look, to what our preferences are, to what we like to eat. They're normal! Usually, these thoughts are undercurrents and don't take up a lot of our emotional time or energy. They don't lead to depression or cause us major anxiety. However, if we have set someone on the throne of our heart, these kinds of thoughts can *overwhelm* us, and cause us to be trapped in a cage of relentless, loud accusation.

But, when God is on the heart- throne, others can reject us without it causing a deep level of pain.

If you're experiencing rejection, it's only because you have not yet understood your full acceptance.

Where does our acceptance come from? Only one place. Ephesians 1:6 says, "... *He made us accepted into the Beloved."* If you have declared Jesus as Lord of your life, you're a brand-new creation in Christ. All the old things and ways have passed away- forever forgotten. We made it!

We're acceptable! We're not trying to behave better to be acceptable to God, *we are acceptable now!* In the truest sense, fullness of acceptance *only comes* from God.

It's from this place of absolute acceptance from God that we can then begin to approach other human relationships. After all, Jesus said that we would love others as we love ourselves. This means that the degree with which we have experientially accepted the acceptance of God, is the same degree that we will accept our spouses, children, friends and others. If you subconsciously feel rejected by God, you will subsequently reject others.

---

*If you subconsciously feel rejected by God,*
*you will subsequently reject others.*

---

I want to make sure I pause here and really make this point well: if you are feeling rejected in any of your relationships, it is because you have not made God alone your anchor point of acceptance, and you have in some way allowed human opinion to rule. There is only one throne on your heart, *and it must always be occupied by God.*

---

*There is only one throne on your heart, and*
*it must always be occupied by God.*

---

Are you feeling rejected by someone? The truth is, you've let them rule you.

When a person's opinion of you takes first place in your heart, they begin to rule you. You start to only be doing as well as that person thinks you are doing well. If you do something they disapprove of, you will find yourself beginning to experience feelings of self- hate, rejection, and isolation.

Then something crazy starts to happen: you will start to conform yourself into the image *that they think* you should be. You will start trying hard to be someone you are not to earn their approval or their favor. You'll change your lifestyle, habits, ways of dressing or speaking to satisfy the demand they placed on you.

The result? You start looking more like them than looking like you, and the authentic image of God that you are *is lost.* You become a copy of an idol instead of the perfectly unique masterpiece that you already are designed to be.

Studies show that nearly 40% of adults report their self-worth is significantly tied to the approval of others. Furthermore, in the age of social media, "comparison anxiety" has led to a 70% increase in reported feelings of "imposter syndrome" among young professionals over the last decade. This proves that "Lordship" isn't just a church word; *it's a mental health necessity*.

I had a childhood friend who wanted me to join her swimming team when I was young. I didn't want anything to do with water and swimming. However, because my friend liked it, I decided to like it. I joined the team and had a horrible year comparing myself to her. She won a lot of races and was very good at her sport. I was often last and didn't have the body composition to do well at that sport. What did I do? I forced my desires to do what she desired to do, and it caused me to do things I would never do to please her. I was outside my comfort zone, and well outside my area of expertise. It produced shame and feelings of insecurity and never being good enough.

If you let the other person's opinion change you, the pain will never stop. Because the identity you're trying to wear was never meant to fit you, you'll become calloused and hard. A hard, calloused heart left untended will eventually lead to you being a shadow of who you once were. A sense of a loss of yourself will grow larger, and the more you try to stuff the pain down, the more self-hate and rejection you will begin to experience.

- You may feel a heaviness, depression, or "slave" mentality.
- You may feel like you're walking around in a cloud, unsure of who you are.
- You may feel like you're an imposter.
- You may feel like you're going through an identity crisis.

All these warning signs are indicators that you have let someone else sit on the throne of your heart.

It is imperative to guard the throne of your heart with diligence and intentionality. Never allow anyone or anything to usurp the place that belongs solely to God. By anchoring your identity and acceptance in the unchanging love of the Holy Spirit, you will find true peace and confidence. This alignment will empower you to navigate human relationships with grace and resilience, free from the bondage of seeking validation from others. Remember, God's acceptance is the ultimate affirmation your heart needs.

None of this is just personal maintenance. When Holy Spirit sits on the throne of your heart, you become safe for other people. You stop needing them to manage your identity, which means you stop unconsciously asking them to carry something they were never meant to carry. One person with a rightly ordered heart-throne changes the relational ecosystem around them. This is how Jesus' prayer in John 17 gets answered — not all at once, from the top down, but one surrendered heart at a time.

# CHAPTER TEN

# The Heart Throne

When using the self-pay grocery checkout line, I hold my breath every time I scan an item. I know that if that item doesn't land in the bag area well enough (or if I remove the bag too quickly), the machine will stop working and demand that I put the item in the bag. It refuses to function without the checkout attendant coming and putting in the manager's code. I can't tell you how many times I've had to wait to have the manager's ok so I can continue checking out! The self- checkout line is very weight- sensitive.

Our hearts were also designed to carry a very precise, certain weight. It's not a grocery store item weight, but it is a unit of measurement concerning weight. However, just like the grocery store checkout cannot function correctly if the wrong weight is on it, so also does the human heart cease to function correctly with the wrong weight. If, at any point, we allow a weight on our heart that it was not designed to carry, we start to break down and do not function correctly.

The Glory of the Lord is one of those weights. Have you ever experienced the glory of the Lord? Usually, I experience glory when I am in worship or prayer. The glory realm is when worship has hit such a flow, the weightiness of the presence of God is in the room in a very tangible way. Usually, the weightiness is heavy, and it can press me down into my seat or onto the floor. I've heard about times that the glory is so heavy; people physically cannot get up from the floor for hours.

The word glory in Greek is the word "doxa." The root of our English word "doxology" comes from doxa. Many of us are familiar with the term doxology, which is a hymn of praise. When we sing a doxology, we acknowledge God's infinite, intrinsic worth. It's not just about what others hear about us; it's about recognizing the unspoken manifestation of God's glory. More specifically, this word doxa means the *weightiness* of His essence. Glory is weight.

Col 1:27 says, *"To them God has chosen to make known among the Gentiles the glorious riches of this mystery, which is Christ in you, the hope of glory."* Where has that weighty glory found its' home? In our hearts.

Revelation 4 speaks about the throne room of God. Eleven times in this chapter alone, the word "throne" is used. All the activity in heaven is centered upon one place: the *One* on the throne. When the Apostle John was on the Isle of Patmos, he suddenly went into a vision of God's throne room. He said, "*Immediately I was in the Spirit; and behold, a throne set in heaven, and One sat on the throne*" (Rev. 4:2). The throne room holds four living creatures who constantly cry out, "Holy, holy, holy" (Rev. 4:8).

Jesus prayed in Luke 11 that it would be "on Earth as it is in Heaven." Just like God has a home and throne room in heaven, He also has one in the Earth: your heart. Your heart is a four-chambered organ who pulses to the same beat the four living creatures have. The lud-dub of your heart mirrors the "ho-ly, ho-ly, ho-ly" of the heavens.

You have 24 ribs, and there are 24 elders in the throne room. You have a four chambered heart, and there are four living creatures in the throne room. You have seven ribs that connect to the sternum, and there are seven lamps of fire that burn before the throne in the Heavens. Your body is a living, moving, breathing replica of the Heavens.

Your human heart was designed to be patterned after the heavenly tabernacle: *One* on the throne. There aren't two thrones- because one person must be in charge. There is an absolute truth that we must agree to- *one head.* Colossians

1:18 says, "And he is the head of the body, the church; he is the beginning and the firstborn from among the dead, so that in everything he might have the supremacy." Just as our physical bodies have a head that directs and sustains us, Jesus is the spiritual head of the Church. His authority, guidance, and love flow through every believer.

One of my mentors early in my Christian journey used to always say, "anything with two heads is a monster." It's so very true. Anything that has two opinions will be like a double minded man. James 1:8 says, "*A double minded man is unstable in all his ways.*" Are you feeling unstable in your life right now? Chances are, there's a fight for the throne space of your heart.

Have you ever experienced a period of heaviness? Usually, there's depression, anxiety or sadness associated with this heavy feeling. It brings darkness and it dulls and destroys the authentic "you" that lies underneath the fog. The prophet Isaiah saw that there would be a solution to this heaviness when he prophesied in Isaiah 61:3. He said there would be, "a garment of praise for the spirit of heaviness."

Heaviness is a spirit. It's an oppressive life destroying demonic spirit. It is *not* the glory-weight we were designed to carry! I believe this is why Jesus said, *"Come to me, all you who are weary and burdened, and I will give you rest. Take my yoke upon you and learn from me, for I am gentle and humble in heart, and you will find rest for your souls. For my yoke is easy and my burden is light."* (Matt 11:28-30).

The weight that Jesus offers us is light and easy. Have you ever experienced a deliverance from the wrong mindset in your life? I have been a part of many deliverance sessions where people become free of demonic oppression. I've seen evil spirits leave people and watch their reaction. Most of them say things like: "I feel so light" or "there's no weight on me!" or "I feel so free!" All of them have this sense of absolute relief, freedom and a lightness of heart and clarity in their minds.

Why do people feel so free when demonic influence leaves? Because the throne issue of the heart was dealt with. Turn with me to 2 Corinthians 3:17, where Paul the Apostle describes freedom in the Spirit. He says, "*Where the Spirit of the LORD is, there is freedom.*" Another translation says, "*Where the Holy Spirit is Lord, there is freedom.*"

Who is to sit upon the throne of your heart? The Lord: but specifically *Holy Spirit*. Your heart-throne is perfectly calibrated to handle the weightiness of this Glory, and no other.

---

Who is to sit upon the throne of your heart?

The Lord: but specifically Holy Spirit.

---

Your heart-throne is perfectly calibrated to handle the weightiness of this Glory, and no other. Many people are familiar with the truth that our bodies are now the temple of God. However, it's not just a generic temple for Father, Son and Holy Spirit. Our bodies are specifically temples of one part of the trinity: *temples of Holy Spirit.* "*Or do you not know that your body is the temple of the Holy Spirit, who is in you, whom you have from God, and you are not your own?*" (1 Cor. 6:19).

If indeed you realize that your body houses God the Holy Spirit, you will think differently about how you relate to God's temple. If you're feeling heavy, it's an indication you've come under the yoke of bondage. You may have evil thoughts about someone or can't honestly say that the Holy Spirit is Lord of your life. You may be depressed, perpetually angry or filled with anxiety. You could also be completely unable to control your thought life.

Chances are, somewhere along the way, you've let another sit on the throne of your heart.

## Blame Game

Most people eventually pull away from hurtful relationships because the pain becomes so deep. Who wants to be hurt? No one! Just like nerves are wired all through our body to indicate when something has hurt the flesh, your feelings are indicators that something is relationally wrong when pain is present. It is imperative that you stop to consider the source of the pain so that the relationship is not damaged.

Who is responsible ultimately for the pain? If you find yourself beginning to lift your hand to point a finger at someone else, turn it around and point it at yourself. *You are.* You're the one who let them rule in your heart.

I tell my children all the time that *blame is a sign of sin.* If blame is involved, you can be sure other aspects of sin preceding it. If we go back to the Garden of Eden, in Genesis 3:11-12, look at what Adam's first words were after the fall: "*I heard Your voice in the garden, and I was afraid because I was naked; and I hid myself.... The woman you gave me, she gave me of the tree, and I ate.*" There was a four-step progression that ended in blame.

### Adam's Four- Step Progression

**One**: He was *afraid* because of his exposure.

**Two**: He *hid* himself.

**Three**: He *covered* his own sin.

**Four**: He *blamed* the other person for his own mistake.

**Blame is always a sign of sin.**

What started out the sin- sequence? Fear. Fear led to hiding, covering and then ultimately: blame. This root of fear could be anything- fear of man, fear of the future, fear of failure... the list of fears can go on and on. What was lost at the fall of man was ultimately a fear issue. Perfect love casts out fear.

1 John 4:18 says, "*There is no fear in love; but perfect love casts out fear, because fear involves torment. He who fears has not been made perfect in love.*" When fear of anything other than God is present, torment begins, and perfect love seems absent.

Fear of the Lord will always bring wisdom, and wisdom is the blueprint of our design in God.

Prov. 9:10 says, "*The fear of the LORD is the beginning of wisdom.*" Wisdom in Hebrew is the word "chokmah." Chokmah means: to have skill in an area, to make yourself or show yourself, to teach. That's important because Prov 3:19 says, "*The LORD by wisdom founded the Earth; By understanding, He established the heavens.*" Proverbs 8:22-23 says, "*The LORD possessed me at the beginning of His way, before His works of old. I have been established from everlasting, from the beginning, before there was ever an earth.*"

**The blueprint of Creation was wisdom.**

These are not just the blueprints of the world, but they're also the blueprints of you. Heb 1:3 says, "*He upholds all things by the Word of His power.*" All of creation is held together by Jesus, who is the Word. That includes not only the Earth and everything on the Earth, but also you and I!

Words are blueprints!

Hang on with me, because I'm going a bit deep to explain what really happened at the fall. Fast forward to the New Testament, where we see Jesus talk about sin. The word for sin in Greek is "hamartia," and it means to be "without form." The beginning of the word, *ha* means negative or without, and *martia* means form.

Sin does not mean to miss the mark, as commonly taught, but it literally means to have no form. *Having no form* will subsequently cause you to miss the mark, but that is not the root of the problem!

Things that are unwise produce sin. However, the absence of wisdom is not the problem. The main problem is the loss of our form.

Look what Jesus says in Luke 5:32 MT: *"I didn't come to re-define the self-righteous but those who realize they couldn't get it right by themselves. I came to awaken "sinners' to recognize their authentic identity mirrored in a complete re-aligned mind."* The Mirror Translation notes say this on the word for "sinner:" The word sinner, is the word "hamartolos," from *ha*, negative or without and *meros*, portion or form; thus, to be without your allotted portion or without form, pointing to a disoriented, distorted and bankrupt identity.

In other words, the blueprint that God made you with when He created you had been distorted and lost.

---

*Someone who sins has just lost their original blueprint- their original form.*

---

Someone who sins has just lost their original blueprint-their original form. This is what happened to Adam in the fall. Fear was only allowed to have a place in his heart because he lost his original blueprint when he listened to the enemy's lies. Adam *feared* that his mistake now defined him instead of his sonship defining him. He moved from having a healthy fear of the Lord, where God's opinion was the only one that mattered, to fearing God's rejection.

Before the fruit, he knew he was accepted and enjoyed fellowship with God. However, after deciding to disobey God, he immediately felt unacceptable. I'm sure the devil whispered something like, "You ate the fruit. God will never forgive you now. You're going to have to hide from Him!" and Adam believed it.

Fear of failure will always produce sin because it's rooted in rejection.

---

*Fear of failure will always produce sin because it's rooted in rejection.*

---

What was the second thing that happened when Adam sinned? He hid. People hide themselves when there is pain, because it exposes their part in sin. Don't hide from the fact that you had a part to play in the pain of the relationship or give someone else the responsibility of bringing reconciliation. Expose it for what it is so that the fellowship walk can be restored.

Next, Adam and Eve covered themselves. Gone was their covering of glory, and they found themselves naked. Instead of being able to say, "I'm sorry I was wrong," they instead deflected and chose to try to cover what they did.

Covering yourself looks like not admitting a mistake, joking to try to change the topic, or never revealing to anyone else what truly happened. Any time we try to cover our own mistakes or failures, shame is allowed to remain and wreak havoc in our hearts.

And finally, the last step: blame. Blame is what happens as a natural result of fear, hiding and covering. If someone is blaming someone else, the three steps before it already happened.

Blame looks like pointing the finger when something goes wrong. **At its root, blame is simply a shield for shame**. When Adam said, *'The woman whom You gave to be with me, she gave me of the tree,'* he wasn't just pointing a finger, but he was also trying to find a way to stay 'covered.' Blame is the 'fig leaf' we use to hide our own nakedness by exposing someone else's. It feels like an act of strength or justice, but it is actually a cry of extreme vulnerability from a person who no longer feels safe in the Father's gaze.

---

*At its root, blame is simply a shield for shame.*

---

Blame is the currency of the kingdom of darkness. While God is the restorer who 'lifts up' the weak, the enemy is the 'accuser' who roars in the sanctuary of our relationships. When we blame, we are partnering with that roar. We are choosing to see through the 'Pharisaical lens' of performance and judgment rather than the 'Jesus lens' of mercy and truth. Blame is the evidence that we are currently eating from the Tree of Knowledge—judging who is 'good' and who is 'bad'—rather than receiving life from the Tree of Life.

We only reach for the weapon of blame when we forget the heart of the Vinedresser. We point the finger to stay covered because we've forgotten that His love has already covered us. Blame is simply the fruit of a branch that doesn't realize it's being lifted toward the Light.

Don't ever blame someone else for your own emotions. You oversee how you handle situations, and who you gave authority over your thought life. *No one* can make you think or feel a certain way. You do that to yourself. "What about if someone makes me mad?" you might think. Well, that person does not have authority over your emotions. You can choose to have an angry response, or a peaceful response. The peace of God that passes understanding can live in you to such a degree, you can sleep through a storm.

If you ever find yourself blaming someone else for the way you feel, think, or act, know for certain that you are absolutely, 100% ... wrong. *You are the only one who can make you mad, sad, happy, or motivated.*

Unless we deal with the root of our independence, we will continue to produce the bitter fruit of blame. Blame is the attempt to survive the disruption by sacrificing our union. It is the belief that 'I can only be okay if you are the problem.' But in the 'seamless union' of the Spirit, there is no 'you' and 'me' to be pitted against each other—there is only 'us' in Him.

| The Step | How it looks in my life today |
| --- | --- |
| **Fear** | "If they really knew me, they'd leave." |
| **Hiding** | Avoiding the conversation or the prayer room. |
| **Covering** | Using humor, busy-ness, or religion to mask the pain. |
| **Blame** | "I only acted that way because you did X." |

When sin entered humanity, it began with a separation from God before it was ever a separation between people. What happened to Adam's relationship with God, and his relationship with Eve when this happened? He lost the daily walk with God- but he also lost trust with his spouse. Relationship with man directly corresponds to our relationship with people.

Romans 8:38 tells us what can separate us from the love of God: "*For I am persuaded that neither death nor life, nor angels nor principalities nor powers, nor things present nor things to come, nor height nor depth, nor any other created thing, shall be able to separate us from the love of God which is in Christ Jesus our Lord.*"

Wow- God's love is so powerful and all-reaching... except for one thing that is not on that list: your past. Your past, not delt with in the light of God's love, can separate you because it's *your choice* to expose it to His love.

If you have hidden sin in your heart, or you have hidden past mistakes or regrets, it will cause a separation between you and God, and therefore you and people. The separation isn't on God's part, but it is on your part.

The journey toward emotional and spiritual freedom is deeply tied to the throne of our hearts. Ensuring that the Holy Spirit reigns supreme within us brings clarity, peace, and an unparalleled sense of freedom. It is imperative to expose hidden sins and past traumas to the light of God's love. This vulnerability is the key to true intimacy with Him and with others.

By relinquishing control and allowing God's perfect love to cast out fear, we can dismantle the strongholds of blame, shame, and hidden pain within our lives. As we embrace this, we will find ourselves walking in greater freedom, deeper fellowship, and a more profound understanding of our authentic identity in Christ.

# CHAPTER ELEVEN

## The Governor

In the late 1800's, a man named William Fisher was fighting a battle against pressure in Marshalltown, Iowa. At the time, if you wanted to keep a steam pump from exploding or failing, a human being had to stand there and manually turn a valve, hour after hour.

Fisher spent one grueling night manually regulating a pump to keep his city's water system from total failure. By morning, he was exhausted, but he had an epiphany: the system didn't need more "manpower"—it needed an automatic constant pressure governor.

He went on to invent a device that could sense the pressure and adjust the flow automatically. It didn't need a human to stay awake and worry; the 'governor' was designed to maintain the "oneness" of the system's pressure regardless of the demand.

This invention birthed Fisher Controls, the company my father worked for when I was a young girl. I remember my dad filling his Stanley coffee container to the brim before he left the house. I remember the red brick building and the steady flow of paper that came home every night.

I grew up in the shadow of that invention, never realizing that God wanted to use that very concept to set me free from "trying harder to be good enough" to living with the pace of knowing that Holy Spirit would empower and govern me.

Fisher Controls became a company that changed the world of engineering. Understanding this concept could change your life.

We are tired of being the "manual valve turners" of our own lives. We have been staying up all night, figuratively speaking, trying to regulate our own anger, our own grades, and our own weight. We have been the "might" and the "power" trying to keep the pressure from blowing.

But the Law of the Spirit of Life is God's "Fisher Governor" for the heart. It is the automatic constant pressure regulator of the Kingdom. When you are governed by the Spirit, you don't have to stand over your own heart with a wrench, frantically trying to keep the pressure of life from destroying you. You can finally stop the manual labor of "trying harder" and trust the Government that was designed to keep you constant.

The aspect of the Holy Spirit as the governor of your life is a key to living a fruitful, peaceful life. I want to encourage you to use the phrase in your everyday life as an expression of who is in control. As you use this language, you will gain mastery of who and what is governing your own life.

## Just Try Harder

The "try harder" message was found in the engine room of a Marshalltown, Iowa building, but it's been shouting from our church pulpits for centuries. For as long as I can remember, the message that was shouted from leaders, coaches, heads of businesses, and church systems was "try harder."

***Try harder.***

Didn't get good grades in school? You must not be trying hard enough. Try harder and add in more math problems and pull the all-nighter so you can ace the test. You must get the best grade so you can be in the best college so you can be at the top of your class.

Is the time on your last mile not fast enough? You need to do some sprint work and add extra workouts and do more resistance training. You're lazy and out of shape! Just try a little harder and you'll see results.

You gained weight again? Time to shape up! Stop eating all that junk and start eating all the right things so that you'll look good. If you don't wear a certain size, you'll never fit in and people will judge you for your lack of willpower.

Passed over for the promotion again? You're never going to amount to anything. You need to try harder to get your boss' attention so they can see your value so you'll be promoted!

You keep sinning, and you can't get it right? Double down on your efforts and kick yourself for not getting it right once again. Read the Word more! Memorize more verses! Attend more church services.

The weapons they would use to try to "encourage" were guilt, shame, and condemnation. In fact, I remember speaking with a Christian friend who thought guilt was *used by God* to get their behavior back in order! They had mistaken the 'whip' for the 'Governor.' They thought God was the coach screaming from the sidelines, not the Life-Giver releasing the grace within them.

Does all that "try harder, work more" language sound normal to you? If so, it shouldn't. God says, *"It's not by might, and it's not by power, but its by My Spirit.* (Zechariah 4:6)."

The 'Try Harder' gospel is like a marathon runner who believes the only way to win is to ignore the pain and sprint from mile 1. It's a recipe for a catastrophic 'DNF' (Did Not Finish) Not only do you not finish, but your body will pay the consequences for your decision, and it's not pretty.

We treat our souls like an engine we have to kick-start with our own willpower, unaware that God has a completely different operating system.

Does willpower have any place in the Kingdom of God?

**Yes, but not as the engine.** Willpower is the 'Yes' in our spirit; it is our choice to stay in the grace of Christ. But it was never designed to be the fuel. When willpower tries to be the fuel, we burn out. When willpower becomes the surrender to the Governor of Holy Spirit, we finish the race.

In the world of endurance, scientists talk about the 'Central Governor.' It's a subconscious regulator in the brain that monitors the heart, the lungs, and the muscles. Its job isn't to hold you back. Its job is to keep you from running into total system failure.

And honestly? This is exactly what the Spirit does for us—if we let Him. While the 'Try Harder' system uses the whips of guilt and shame to get us to perform, the Holy Spirit acts as a Divine Governor. He doesn't shout 'Try harder' from the sidelines; He sits on the Heart Throne and regulates the flow of His life through our thoughts and into our behavior.

The Law of Sin is a whip; the Law of the Spirit is a grace impulse in the heart. One drives you from behind with pain; the other leads you from the inside with peace.

The language of the Law that produces sin always says, "try harder." But the language of Grace always says, "He empowers me."

There are two laws that are at work in your life right at this very moment. Paul spoke of them in Romans 7 and 8. One law is the law of sin and death that produces sin and death in your life. The other law is the law of the Spirit of life in Christ, which produces life!

Romans 8:2 says, *"The law of the Spirit of life in Christ Jesus has made me free from the law of sin and death."*

One law produced ten commandments, a cycle of never-ending sacrifices, and generation after generation of rule breaking Pharisees whose hearts were far from God. The other law produced fruitful disciples and apostles like Paul, Peter, and John.

When Jesus came, He fulfilled the law of sin and death. But catch this, because it's amazing news. He fulfilled the law not just of the old system, but *He fulfilled the law in you.*

*"For what the law could not do in that it was weak though the flesh, God did by sending His own Son in the likeness of sinful flesh, on account of sin: He condemned sin in the flesh, that the righteous requirement of the law might be fulfilled in us who do not walk according to the flesh but according to the Spirit."*

-Romans 8:3-4

Did you catch that?! The law has been fulfilled IN YOU!!

This new law that is by the Spirit is the law you now operate under in Christ. What was once an external behavior modification system has now become an *internal government system.*

How do you get free from sin cycles and destruction in your life? Certainly not by trying harder. It's by submitting to the Law of the Spirit of life ***in Christ Jesus.*** You cannot be free of sin apart from the governing power of the Spirit.

In fact, Romans 8 goes on to say that if you live according to the flesh, (in other words, trying to save yourself by your self-effort and willpower, you will die.) However, if by the Spirit you put to death the deeds of the body, you will live! (Romans 8:13). The Holy Spirit is the one who is able to destroy sin, and its works in our hearts by His government.

| The Law of Sin & Death | The Law of the Spirit of Life |
|---|---|
| **Fuel:** Self-Effort / Might | **Fuel:** Grace / The Spirit |
| **Motivation:** Guilt & Shame | **Motivation:** The Father's Embrace |
| **Method:** External Behavior Modification | **Method:** Internal Government |
| **Result:** Burnout & Death | **Result:** Oneness & Life |

## The Bride

Proverbs 31 has long been known because of its description of the perfect woman. Yes, it does an incredible job of describing an amazing Godly woman but remember that we as the Church are also the Bride of Christ. This isn't just a standard for women; it's the standard for the heart of every believer.

One verse from Proverbs 31 has always jumped out at me. Prov 31:26 says, "*She opens her mouth with wisdom and on her tongue is the law of kindness.*"

The *law* of kindness? Yes! Kindness is not a personality trait we try to put on like makeup before we go out into the world! It is a *fruit* of the Spirit. The fully mature Bride of Christ has learned that it's not by her might or her power that she speaks, but by her tongue being governed by a new law.

This law isn't her "biting her tongue," and trying not to sin, but it has *transformed* her tongue!

There have been many times in my life my tongue has not been transformed. In fact, I've often said things out of anger, frustration, or sheer exhaustion that I wish I could take back. Thankfully, my kids are gracious and quick to forgive, and so is my husband.

When I started to meditate on Proverbs 31, I began to see it show up in my everyday life. I began to walk with the awareness that kindness was governing my tongue. When the laundry didn't get done, or when the kids were fighting, or when I made a mistake, I started to notice in my own life in a very real way that *there was change taking place.* I knew there really was something significant was happening to me!

For years, I had always wanted to be a Godly wife or woman. I tried to do it in all the wrong ways. I'm one of the ones who stepped on the scale and had shame. I'm one who doubled down on my workouts or felt horrible about my bad grades. I am now learning to live guided by the Spirit, which has impacted my life more than any textbook or manual. I found a "law" that was the key to everything.

Think about our Proverbs 31 Bride. Kindness has now become a *law* in her life. It's no longer a choice she has to struggle with at the end of a hard day; it is the governed rhythm of her heart. It's no wonder Paul wrote in Romans 2:4 that it is the kindness of God—not the whip of shame—that leads us to repentance. When we are governed by His kindness, our "beet-red fury" is replaced by the Law of Wisdom, which is from the Law of the Spirit of life in Christ.

We will have wisdom in situations to not react in anger, frustration, or resort to mustering up more willpower. We stop trying to "talk ourselves into" being nice and start allowing the Governor to release the fruit that is already growing within us.

What does this look like in our lives? Instead of trying harder to get good grades in school, we allow Holy Spirit to empower us with faithfulness to study and learn. We believe

He is empowering us by teaching us all things, and by giving us wisdom in every area we need it.

Instead of working out harder to make our athletics endeavors more successful, ask Holy Spirit what you should be doing and when. People often overwork their bodies and cause high cortisol and other problems when what they really need is rest!

Instead of getting on the scale, and condemning yourself by hating your body, thank God for your body and begin to love it. *You can never change something you hate.* Being kind to yourself will cause you to change your behavior.

The finish line of the "Try Harder" gospel is always burnout, but the starting line of the Law of the Spirit is acceptance of His Lordship. You were never meant to be the engineer of your own holiness or the frantic mechanic of your own heart. You were meant to be enthroned by the One who makes all things new.

You don't have to reach for willpower the next time you can feel the tension rising inside you. Instead, gently remind your heart it's now under a new Governor: the Holy Spirit.

And here's why this matters beyond just your own peace: a Church governed by the Spirit looks completely different from a Church governed by the law of sin and death. When believers stop white-knuckling their way through holiness and start living from the inside out, something corporate begins to shift. The unity Jesus prayed for isn't forged by effort and agreement — it's the natural overflow of people who have each, individually, let the Governor take the wheel.

# CHAPTER TWELVE

# When Sin Remains Hidden

I had something incredibly traumatic happen to me in college. It was so traumatic that I was never able to tell anyone what happened to me. Over time, I would share small facts that were more "big picture," but for almost 20 years, I held the trauma all to myself. It was too shameful, dark and ugly to share.

Hiding things never goes well. As time went by, one of my friends and I became close. Years into our relationship, we began to open to one another about things that had scared us and wounded us in our past. One day, I began to tell her some of the details of what I went through. To that point, I had not yet told my husband.

I left the meeting that day feeling a cross between relief that the "secret" was exposed, but a trembling that now someone else knew. If my friend wanted to, she could deeply wound me with her newfound information. However, this friend that I have sticks closer than a brother, and because of the way she honors me, she has kept my secret trauma safe.

Years later, she helped me begin to understand that my husband needed to know what happened to me. After wrestling it out with the Lord, I knew that it was important that I share not just part of my life with my husband, but all the events that have made me who I am. I think the timing was perfect, because we had both grown to a place of maturity, he could handle me telling him. I think if I had told him earlier, it would not have gone well. This needed to be a conversation that began by being led by the Holy Spirit.

When I told my husband what happened, it opened a very deep place of love that neither of us had experienced before, but also deep pain. I was stunned that my husband in some ways re-lived what I went through- in shock and disbelief. He had a hard time coming to grips with it all, and it was a process to walk it out together.

My husband was also able to share some things with me that he had never told anyone. After a few days of dealing with the new information, we both felt peace, freedom, and much deeper level of fellowship in our marriage. He had a new respect for me, and I him. We both understood one another more completely.

What we chose to do was very vulnerable. One of the key aspects of intimacy is vulnerability. Many people often shrink away from the word "vulnerable" because of painful experiences in their past. However, vulnerability is the golden key for unlocking any kind of deep and lasting relationship. Did you just shudder? Don't worry, I know what that feels like.

For a long time in my life, I shut up all my deep, dark secrets, because I feared I would not be accepted if I shared. I covered myself, refusing to let any kind of vulnerability crack my hard shell of self-protection. I did not know that it was doing much more harm than good.

Vulnerability is intimacy. A way of looking at the word "intimacy" is "into me see." Intimacy is a transaction in which you are giving another person permission to see how you think, feel, and process events or information. It is the "uncovering" of who you are to another. You let them see all the parts of which you are unsure, embarrassed, or afraid.

Embracing vulnerability and allowing ourselves to be seen by others is a transformative journey. It is through this exposure that we build deeper connections and grow in trust. The choice to open and share our hearts is not a sign of weakness, but a courageous step towards genuine intimacy and emotional freedom. As you navigate your relationships, be discerning about who you share your deepest thoughts with, and trust that in the right context, vulnerability can lead to a stronger bond with trusted friends and family around you.

## You Can't Share Your Heart With Just Anyone

One day, I met a friend at a coffee shop. She and I were discussing the deep things of the Lord, and I was sharing some things that God was showing me in prayer. Suddenly, a mutual acquaintance came into the shop and sat down with us. She began telling us a story about something with her mother, and I immediately began sharing the wisdom the Lord had given me that morning in prayer.

I could tell that what I was sharing was not well received. However, I knew that what I was sharing had the potential to turn her whole situation around for the better. I mean, God had *just* spoken it to me! It must have been for her! Undeterred, I continued sharing as she stared back at me with a blank face.

Shortly after, I left the shop and began the drive home. I felt uncomfortable and sour inside. Even though I knew what I shared was Biblical and applicable, the acquaintance had not received it, and in fact, seemed offended by what I had to share. I began to feel shame about sharing my pearls.

I got home and began to speak to the Lord about what had just happened. "Why do I feel so awful, Lord? Was that not

You showing me these things? Was I not supposed to share?"

Immediately, I thought of King Hezekiah, when he welcomed the Babylonian embassy into Israel, and showed all the treasures of his kingdom. The Babylonians were not friends of Israel, and it was Hezekiah's pride that caused him to boast about what he had. 2 Kings 20:13 says, "*And Hezekiah received the envoys and showed them all that was in his treasure house—the silver, the gold, the spices, and the fine olive oil—his armory and everything found among his treasures. There was nothing in his palace or in all his kingdom that Hezekiah did not show them."*

Unfortunately, because Hezekiah shared pearls with someone who should not have seen them, there were grave consequences. Hezekiah's descendants were taken into captivity, and everything that he showed them was carried off to Babylon.

It is unwise to share the deep pearls of wisdom that the Lord has given you with just anyone. Many times, they are not wanted, and unwelcome. Everyone should not know everything about you. Oversharing can be a huge stumbling block and produce a lot of pain. Knowing who to share information with requires discernment.

Jesus warned us not to throw pearls before swine. It's not that the people are 'pigs,' but that they don't have the 'digestive system' (the maturity) to handle the value of what you're giving them. They will only trample the treasure and turn to tear you.

It is a good and right thing to be able to share what you're learning with others! Sharing with others your pain and joys are biblical. However, when you choose to share these very tender parts of your heart and history with people, you must consider the person you are talking to. I have one friend who is very gifted in mercy. She has the amazing ability to sympathize with and bring comforting words, gifts and even food to people who are really struggling. That's not an area that I excel in by any means, so I'm not the best person to help if she has questions about her gifting.

I have another friend who has been incredibly hurt in previous friendships because they've shared too much, too deeply. This friend, I am unable to go as deep with because of the boundaries that they put up. Over time, trust develops. But this can take a great deal of time.

If the person we are bringing our vulnerability to has not matured in Christ to the point that they can help us with our problems, the conversation has great potential to produce pain instead of healing. You will most likely end up walking away hurt, because they didn't- and they can't- understand you. As beautiful, powerful, and life-giving intimacy can be it can also be incredibly painful. Rejection, judgement and hurt can easily be the product of interactions between friends.

It is always a good idea to test new friendships with a small amount of disclosure and see how well the other person handles the information you share with them. If people are responsible with little, they can possibly be entrusted with more of your heart. This is wisdom! Trust develops slowly over time, and with investment.

One of the best definitions of the word "trust" I've ever heard came from a theologian named Karl Bart. He said, "Trust is the courage to accept that you are accepted." Trust is a *must* for any healthy intimate relationship.

But and this is a big but- that accepting trust must originate *first* in God.

*We must have wisdom to know who to share our heart with, and how much of our heart to share.* Of course, we can tell Jesus everything, but there is something powerful that happens when you confess parts of your heart to another human. This is why James 5:16 says, "*Confess your trespasses to one another, and pray for one another, that you may be healed. The effective, fervent prayer of a righteous man avails much.*" Confession brings healing, and you may need that friend to intercede for you.

Above all, the human heart was designed to first have Lordship and intimacy with the Holy Spirit. As we navigate life, we must do it first through Holy Spirit's leadership, and then through words from trusted friends or family members.

To wrap things up, being vulnerable and forming deep connections with others requires discernment, bravery, and trust. It's about knowing when and with whom to share our innermost thoughts and experiences. True intimacy is built on mutual respect and understanding. While it's important to open the heart and share, it's equally vital to be selective about who we confide in. By doing this, we can build strong, meaningful relationships that can truly transform our lives, with genuine love and connection.

# CHAPTER THIRTEEN

# Breaking the Power of Shame and Secrets

Secrets are always rooted in shame. They are secrets for that very reason. A secret is something that is covered, hidden, and unexposed. The only reason people try to cover their mistakes is because they do not understand that the blood of Jesus over their mistake *is their covering*. This is why Adam and Eve hid in the garden: they tried to cover themselves to prevent their sin- secret from being exposed.

Have you seen the movie, Inside Out 2? In the movie, the young teenage girl, Riley, has a "deep, dark secret." In the movie, this giant, who lives behind her "secret vault," is hiding in there because he is her deepest, darkest secret. This secret is so seriously bad, he cannot ever be let out of the vault. Later in the movie, we find out what this horrific secret is: Riley is ashamed that she burnt a hole in a rug. This is a "face-palm" moment.

You or I can look at that and think, "That's silly. Who cares about that? It's not like she murdered someone!" The truth is the deep, dark secrets we have only have their power because *we think* they are powerful. They really are no big deal at all, but when they are kept in the dark, they feel like a big deal. When they are exposed to the light, they lose all their power to keep you in fear or torment.

When we have friendships that have deeper levels of vulnerability in them, these "deep, dark secrets" have an escape route. The combination to the vault must be entered, the door swung open, and that secret exposed. *You cannot reveal your secrets to just anyone*! You must have wisdom enough not to splatter all your secrets on Facebook. On the other hand, you must have enough wisdom to know that you can't hold it in, keeping it a secret.

Hopefully, you have a trusted friend in which this exchange can take place. A trusted friend, who accepts you, loves you, and wants the best for you is the ideal person. You can open that vault in your heart and begin to share the thing that you've never told anyone before.

Often, that "deep, dark secret" is holding you in bondage, and has destroyed your life by causing you to believe a lie about yourself. My husband, daughters, and friends have all shared with me things they have "never told anyone." Every single one of those secrets they had to tell me was just part of doing life- things that every single person at one point or other struggles with.

If a person is keeping a sin-secret, they are harboring the enemy inside the temple of God. That secret will eat away at them and have the power to distort many areas of thinking. If the secret is a secret, there will be some level of bondage with a guilty conscience, and it has the power to completely change a person's life.

A single hurtful comment from a classmate was etched in my heart as a teenager. They said, "you're so big. You're the biggest girl there is." In truth, I was. I've always been tall and big boned. I could have ignored the comment, embraced myself and thanked God for how He made me, but I didn't know how to do that. Instead, I took that comment, and it grew inside my heart until all I could hear was the enemy screaming, "you're worthless unless you're small. If you want to be accepted, you must be the same size as other people."

If I had only been able to recognize the comment as a lie and a distortion of my identity, I might have stopped the harmful lie from taking root in my heart.

I couldn't make myself shorter, but I could make myself skinnier. That single lie catapulted me into a full-blown eating disorder for over fifteen years. Because of it, I lost my basketball college scholarship, spent thousands of dollars on eating disorder treatment, and years of my life to a soul-eating lie that I allowed to almost kill me.

*Allowing that single thought to remain could have destroyed me.*

What would have happened if I had opened my heart to someone and told them that that one lie had gotten out of control, and I needed help? That comment became a secret I kept in my heart on lockdown because of how worthless it made me feel. I was full of shame for how God created me. Did that one person's comment have the right to define me? No, but sadly I was completely ignorant of the truth that could set me free. I don't want you to be as ignorant and trapped as I was.

The enemy will try to set up traps for you with the goal of your utter destruction. He will tempt you with lies that will seem like truth because there may be a partial truth in them. If you choose to believe a lie, it will prevent you from reaching your God-given potential. He will siderail you, try to slow you down, discredit you, shame you, and hijack your identity. All these things are just his whispers to get you to stop moving forward in God.

How did I get free? I began to read the Word of God, and I started to learn how to pray. If you do not know what the Word says about who God is, or who you are, you will greatly struggle- constantly looking to please the opinions and the culture around you. John 8:32 says, "And you shall know the truth, and the truth shall make you free." Jesus, the man, is the truth.

If you are having a hard time finding a way of escape from your past or trauma, let me point you in the right direction: *Jesus is the way out.* John 14:6 says, "Jesus said to him, '*I am the way*, the truth, and the life..." (author's emphasis). He is truth, and as you get to know Him, you will be set free and find life, and life abundantly.

Secrets do not define who we are unless you believe them and allow them to define you. God defines who we are! Until the secret is released, the enemy has the power to keep reminding and accusing people of lies. Once the secret is let out, light can flood our souls, and we are free to be who God has called us to be- free of the controlling, accusing voice of the enemy. Being able to be vulnerable and letting your guard down with a trusted friend could change your life.

If someone asks you to keep a secret, let them know that won't be possible. Usually, secrets relate to shame. They are a means to "cover up" what needs to be exposed. Secrets always keep people in prison. The enemy always *seeks agreement* to confirm the lie and make it masquerade as the truth. If you agree with their secret, you've just helped secure both you and them in a locked chamber. You may feel pressure and fear the loss of the relationship if you choose not to keep the secret.

People need to be able to talk through complex emotional issues freely with trusted, specific friends. It's not your job to spread gossip or false information, but don't come to an agreement with keeping things in the dark. (Unless it's a Christmas present. Those are fine!).

## God Shares His Secrets with His Friends

Did you know that God has secrets, too? He doesn't *keep* secrets, but He has them *hidden for us*! God's secrets are like tiny treasures He has hidden for us. God wants to share them, because that's what loving intimacy does. He *loves* being able to share them with His friends. These secrets are never associated with shame and are very different from human trauma.

God doesn't share His secrets with just anybody. There are some specific people that He will share His secrets with. Psalm 25:14 says, "The *secret* of the LORD is with those *who fear Him*, and He will *show them* His covenant."

Let's break these three phrases down:

1. **Secret**: The word "secret" in that verse is the Hebrew word "cowd." It means, "a session, a company of persons in close, deliberate discussion- by implication: intimacy." Secret is really the word for intimacy! God's secrets are reserved for those who are intimate with Him. Secrets are usually referred to as *revelations* from God.

2. **Fear Him:** The phrase "who fear Him" is the word "yare"- and it means to revere- to be in reverence. Proverbs 9:10 tells us that the fear of

the Lord is the beginning of wisdom. If you want to be wise, pay attention to this next part!

Often, we will go to a friend for wise counsel. This friend may give us some advice or speak about the matter. What they have to say may or may not be true, but it is up for consideration if you need help. Asking for council is wise- because in a multitude of counselors there is wisdom (Prov. 15:22). However, be careful because this can lead to a trap.

One of the traps you can fall into is to begin to fear man's opinion over the opinion of God. When you ask for advice, you will get feedback on what your friend thinks. That feedback is just a person's opinion *until* the Word of God comes in support of what was said. If we don't take that friend's feedback back to the Word of God, we can potentially make a grievous error.

Intimacy is authority. Whoever you are intimate with, you empower to have a voice to speak into your life. Ultimately, intimacy brings a level of control. This control can either be of the flesh or of the Spirit. Romans 8:6 says, "For the sense and reason of the flesh is death, but the mindset controlled by the Holy Spirit brings life and peace." The advice born of flesh and sense and reason will ultimately produce death. You may feel manipulated, used, or feel shame.

However, in the Kingdom, this intimate authority to control us is beautifully expressed as our minds being controlled by the Holy Spirit. That's where we want to be!

Your friend is not God, and although many times our friends have keys that unlock doors of revelation for us, they should never be given *authority* to rule over your life. We cannot live lives that are full of wisdom if we are constantly looking at people to tell us if what we are doing is right or wrong. Once you let someone in and give them the power to tell you what to do, the *fear of man* has been given a place on the throne of your heart.

If you are afraid that your friend will leave you, think less of you, or reject you for not receiving their advice, fear of man has set in your heart. If you feel like you must agree with them to have them approve of you, fear of man has set in your heart. If you feel like you need their approval to do well in life, fear of man has control of your heart.

Fear of the Lord and fear of man cannot exist at the same time. There is only one throne in your heart, and what you fear will sit upon that throne. Not only will the fear of man sit upon the throne ruling you, but it also will cause more fear of man to come upon you. Job 3:11 says, *"For the thing which I greatly feared is come upon me, and that which I was afraid of is come unto me."*

Ultimately, *who you fear* will have authority over your life.

---

*Ultimately, who you fear will have authority over your life.*

---

I promise you- there is only ONE opinion that matters, and it's not yours or your friends. It's God's! The secret of the Lord is with those *who fear Him.*

3. **He Will Show Them:** The phrase "He will show them" is the word "yada." Yada is to know by seeing something. It carries with it a two-part experience: seeing and letting that "seeing" become understanding. For example, if someone shows us a new plant, but we only know the name and have not seen what it looks like, we have not fully experienced the plant. Only by knowing the name and seeing it can we describe to another what it is like and fully appreciate its beauty.

We don't know God until we have seen Him. That's why it was imperative that Jesus came to the Earth as a human. It's only in Jesus that we have seen what God the Father is like. John 14:9 says, "If you've seen Me, you've seen the Father."

I'm not talking about seeing God with just with our human eyes (although some people have seen visions of Jesus in dreams or while praying), I'm talking about the eyes of our spirit. In Ephesians 1:8, Paul prays that the "eyes of your understanding would be enlightened, that you would know the hope of His calling, and what are the riches of the glory of His inheritance in the saints." Without our spiritual eyes *seeing* the Father, we will never have hope of a calling or know about Jesus's (and subsequently our) inheritance.

"Seeing God" happens when we experience the Word (Jesus) coming to life in our times of prayer, worship, meditation, or communion. When we pray, we must know that He doesn't share His secrets with people who do not see Him in prayer.

I once had a friend come to visit my house. She asked me, "Just out of curiosity- why don't you have any pictures of Jesus in your home?" I was a little stunned by her question because it had never crossed my mind before. After I thought about it, I said, "Because I don't need a picture of someone that I see all the time. We only have pictures of those who come and go or those who grow to remember a specific time or place. I'm face to face with Him all the time, whenever I want. That- and all the artists renderings I've seen make Jesus look different than I see Him. I don't want a picture to ruin the Face that I know and love."

How do we see Him? We see Him face to face. The word that the New Testament uses to describe not only Jesus' prayer life, but ours is the word *proseuchomai* in Greek. Pros, the root word, is a word that means, "face to face- towards, with, or in the presence of." *Euchomai* is the verb "to speak out/ to utter." So together, proseuchomai means to pray face to face with God. Here are some examples of where proseuchomai is used:

- *"Rejoice always, pray without ceasing, in everything give thanks; for this is the will of God in Christ Jesus for you."* (1 Thessalonians 5:16-18)
- *"Be anxious for nothing, but in everything by prayer and supplication, with thanksgiving, let your requests be made known to God; and the peace of God, which surpasses all understanding, will guard your hearts and minds through Christ Jesus."* (Philippians 4:6-7)
- *Then Jesus came to a place called Gethsemane, and said to the disciples, "Sit here, while I go pray."* (Matt. 26: 36)
- *"Continue earnestly in prayer, being vigilant in it with thanksgiving."* (Colossians 4:2 (NKJV)
- *"Therefore, I say to you, whatever things you ask when you pray, believe that you receive them, and you will have them."* (Mark 11:24 NKJV)
- *"Rejoicing in hope, patient in tribulation, continuing steadfastly in prayer."* (Romans 12:12)
- *"But at midnight Paul and Silas were praying and singing hymns to God, and the prisoners were listening to them."* (Acts 16:25)
- *"But you, when you pray, go into your room, and when you have shut your door, pray to your Father who is in the secret place; and your Father who sees in secret will reward you openly."* (Matthew 6:6)

This is just a small sample. I found over 112 scriptures that use proseuchomai to describe prayer. Repeatedly in scripture, prayer is used in the context of being face to face with God. God shares intimacy with those who reverently worship Him by seeing Him face to face as He speaks.

This face-to-face posture isn't just for nothing. Something happens as we are face to face with Him. As my friend Daniela and I were discussing this word one day, she shared with me that at the Mount of Transfiguration, Jesus modeled what that face-to-face experience produced. Luke 9:29 says: *"As He was praying, the appearance of his face was transformed, and His clothes became dazzling white."* Why was the appearance of His face transformed?

When Jesus prayed, He was a model for what happens when we pray. The word used to describe Jesus' prayer was – you guessed it- *proseuchomai.* To pray is to intimately move towards God, towards him, face to face. Transformation took place as Jesus prayed! *As Jesus prayed*, which we know is to move intimately towards the Father, face to face, breath to breath, the appearance of His face transformed.

What happens when we engage in prayer, when the body of Christ engages into prayer? Transformation! Look at what 2 Corinthians 3:18 says: "*But we all, with unveiled face, beholding as in a mirror the glory of the Lord are being transformed into the same image from glory to glory, just as by the Spirit of the Lord.*"

Jesus took Peter, James, and John, his intimate ones to witness what happened when he prayed. When we pray in the Face of Jesus, in the face of the Father *we are transformed*! Do you now see why prayer is so vital personally and corporately?

## Jesus' Model

Jesus modeled friendship and relationships perfectly. He was able to walk through life victorious because He was fueled by His Father's *absolute acceptance*. Before He ever did a single miracle, teaching, healing or ministry work, He received words of affirmation and acceptance from His Father. He waited for the Father to say, "*This is my beloved Son, in whom I am well pleased.*" (Matt 3:17). If God the Son waited for God the Father to voice His acceptance before He did any public ministry, how much more so do we?

Before we do anything publicly at all, we must begin at acceptance and then move into action. Fatherly *acceptance* fueled Jesus' ability to make disciples, do works of ministry, and fully obey His Father.

That acceptance for Jesus is full. In whole fullness, He was not lacking in a sense of identity. He never looked to his natural parents, friends, or disciples for a sense of completeness or praise. In fact, Jesus said in John 5:41, *"I do not receive glory from men."* The word for glory is "doxa," and is also translated as "praise" or "worship." Of course, humans worship Jesus- but He never receives it. He always lived to glorify the Father. *The praise went right through Him, to another.*

Imagine the heart as a window, not a mirror. A mirror catches the light and keeps it (pride); a window lets the light pass through to the Father (freedom).

Jesus knew that the moment he received the praise of men, it would sit on the throne of His heart instead of His Father. This left us the picture of a fully complete man of God: he could receive encouragement but never let it affect his heart-throne.

The proof of this is when Judas betrayed Him. Jesus knew that Judas's kiss was an intimate betrayal by a close friend. And yet, *He did not experience rejection.* In fact, Jesus was so secure in His love and acceptance from Abba, that He could say this to Judas: "friend, why have you come?" (Matt. 26:50). If we can't call our betrayer "friend," it's because we still value their opinion more than God's.

Think of the last time someone close to you betrayed you. Could you have gone to them and called them, "friend" in your darkest hour of rejection? If the answer is "no," then it's an indication of a problem. Perhaps you've enthroned them in your heart. The evidence of the enthronement is the presence of painful rejection. *If you've enthroned them, you most likely worship their opinion of you. Subsequently, this allows that person to be your god.*

Receiving praise from people allows them access to your heart-throne. From that moment on, you only feel stable and secure if they approve of you. The moment that you do something they don't like or disagree with; you will begin to feel their rejection. This can only happen because *you* made the decision to put them on the throne.

The rejection that you subsequently feel then fuels conflict.

At times, people will naturally give you compliments or bring words of encouragement and support along your life journey. It is good and right that people do this! However, we must model what Jesus showed us. You don't take those comments to heart as if you yourself have done those things, but you let the compliment flow right through you to glorify God.

If the compliment is left only with you, there is a great chance it will remain in your heart and take root as pride. If you continually receive compliments from a certain source, and then the person stops complimenting you and turns on you, it will produce a deep wound of rejection.

To give the praise and compliment to the Lord keeps your heart free to love, just like Jesus did. Let the praise go right through you, to God- to Whom it is ultimately due.

This is the work that makes oneness possible at a corporate level. It is slow, it is hidden, and it is rarely celebrated. But a church full of people who have brought their secrets into the light — who have nothing left to protect and nothing left to hide — is a church that can actually be one. Transparency doesn't threaten unity. It's the very ground unity grows in.

# CHAPTER FOURTEEN

# Unity

The fuming anger from my husband was palpable. I was furious, and the rage I felt built up in me like a pot about to boil over. He was livid, and his face was beet red. I remember wanting with everything inside of me to run away and never have to see him ever again. It seemed like we had come to an impasse in our marriage where we simply were not going to agree, and the chasm might as well have been a billion miles wide. Have you been there?

Marital fights are never fun. Although few and far between these days, our early days of marriage were horrendous, and the fights were really heated. The day we got married, we made each other an extra vow: we vowed that we would never say the "d" word: divorce. We knew that God hates divorce, and that there would be times we would be tempted to leave the marriage.

Gen 2:24 says, *"Therefore a man shall leave his father and mother and be joined to his wife, and they shall become one flesh."* God created man and woman *to become one*, and we never- no matter how bad things got- wanted to split what God joined together.

God took two beings who look quite different from the outside, and made them a perfect, complimentary match. *He made them one.*

Marriage reflects Christ and the church (Eph 5:31), but this idea of two becoming one is much larger and more in depth than just human marriage. Focus on the marriage being of two parts- which are very different- coming together to make one. This theme repeats itself in other ways in scripture.

Let's go back to the very beginning, when God created the first two things: Heaven and Earth. (Gen. 1:1.) Heaven and Earth had been two very distinctly different places until Jesus came on the scene and prayed, "Let it be on Earth as it is in Heaven." His words were a prayer that would bring two seemingly contrary realities together into one reality: oneness.

Those realities are not contrary, but complementary.

Christ and the Church, man and woman, Heaven and Earth, and Jew and Gentile are all scriptural examples of "two becoming one."

To look at this truth a little more closely, we're going to consider how God made Jew and Gentile one in Christ. The Jewish people were God's chosen nation- a people who God called out of pagan culture to learn His ways. Gentiles were any other people group in the Earth. Until Jesus came, Yahweh God was only the God of the Jewish people. However, Jesus came to make the two become one. He came to announce that Gentiles, or unbelievers, were also included in salvation.

In many ways, this is a mystery, but Paul clears up some of that mystery in his letter to the Church at Ephesus. Paul was instructing the Ephesian Church how to get along- and it's no wonder, because the church was predominately made of Gentile converts, as well as Jewish people. How do you help these two groups understand that God designed them to operate as one?

To understand this, I want you to stop here and think about a time when you were in a damaged relationship. Perhaps, it was a horrible fight in your marriage. Maybe, the damage was with a best friend, or a co-worker. Like the pain I felt in the fight with my husband, can you feel that distance and just wanting to run away and hide? Perhaps you've even felt this way about God.

Now I want you to read this next verse:

*Ephesians 2:13-18 says, "But now in Christ Jesus you who were once far away have been brought near by the blood of Christ."*

Go back and read the verse again. I want you to really slow down, close your eyes, and imagine the blood of Christ bringing close the person who was at one point far away from you. Consider these words heavily: "You who were once *far away* have been *brought near* by the blood of Christ."

The Cross didn't just span the gap between us and God; it spans the gap between the 'billion-mile chasm' of a marital fight. When we look through the blood, the distance vanishes because the blood has already paid for the peace.

The blood of Christ is powerful enough to bring a sinner back to reconciliation with God Himself. *He is abl*e to bring human-to-human reconciliation as well.

At one point in our marriage, things were very difficult and volatile. However, we have both grown so much in wisdom and love that we greatly enjoy one another. We have learned not to blame, but to take responsibility for our own behavior. Every year we are married, our marriage becomes richer and fuller. We are continually discovering new depths in one another.

The unity Jesus purchased with His blood can transform our relationships and marriages. By doing so, we foster environments where peace, understanding, and seamless oneness can thrive. God has placed us in families and relationships to represent Himself in the Earth. Because He filled us with His power, we can be peacemakers, and His blood has the power to destroy even the strongest separations.

## Vision for Marriage

I had a friend tell me about an encounter that she had with a minister named Mylon LeFevre, who has since gone to be with the Lord. She had an opportunity to talk with Mylon and asked him about his marriage. She could tell that he and his wife had a very unusual dynamic between the two of them. He began to share the difference between unity and agreement. He said that the unity in his marriage was like seamless oneness. He said, "I know how she's going to respond and what she will say about anything at any given time, because we are *one*." This conversation happened years ago, but she felt the anointing so strong on the conversation, she's spoken to me about it several times over the years. Is it possible to be that close... to be one?

Unless you have a vision for it, it's very difficult to grasp.

Being able to see where God wants our marriage to grow to is instrumental to experiencing greater levels of unity and peace with one another. Proverbs 29:18 says, *"Where there is no vision, the people perish..."* If we don't know where we're headed, how can we have successful growth? We need to know what the ultimate expression of true marriage looks like in its end goal so that we can move towards the goal.

One thing that greatly aided my ability to see my marriage correctly was the revelation of unity inside Adam and Eve *before the fall.*

The Old Testament was originally written entirely in Hebrew. A little bit about the Hebrew language: Hebrew doesn't contain any capital or lowercase letters. Hebrew is written largely with abjad script and has only 22 letters in it, and each letter only has one form, regardless of its position in a word.

Let's zero in on the word "man" in Hebrew. God created man in Genesis 2:7, and it's the first time that the word "man" appears. In Genesis chapters 2 and 3, the Hebrew word *adam* (אָדָם), which is often translated as "man" or "Adam," appears 11 times. This word is used to refer to the first human being created by God, *as well as* mankind in general.

In Genesis 2:21-24, God created woman out of man. The word "woman" is *'ishshah,* and it means "female, together, wife, or woman."

So, we have 'adam, symbolizing all of humanity, and ishshah, who was made *from* man's ('adam's) rib. Here's where it gets interesting: Adam said, "This is now bone of my bones and flesh of my flesh; She shall be called Woman, Because she was taken out of Man."

Adam saw Eve as being *part of himself.* We know this, because in the next verse, God said, "Therefore a man shall leave his father and mother and be joined to his wife, and they shall become *one flesh.*"

The word "one" there is the Hebrew word 'echad. It literally means One: a single unit, united, or unity. The root word means "to bring together."

Adam had called Eve "woman," but at this point in the historical account, *Eve did not have the name Eve.* She was only known as "woman," and bone of Adam's bone and flesh of his flesh. Remember that Hebrew has no capital letters? Our English bible has Adam's name capitalized, but it's still *just the root word for "all of mankind."*

Genesis 3 records the temptation and fall of man. As the woman and man hid from God, the Lord God called out to 'adam and said, "Where are you?" Now, in the Hebrew, that word isn't capitalized, and we can't separate out if that was Adam's proper name, or if God was calling to all mankind. I believe that when God went through the garden, *He was calling to them both.*

I believe this because God made 'adam in His own image. God is three parts: Father, Spirit and Son, but all three are in perfect oneness. Just as you could separate out 'adam from 'ishshah, so could you separate out the functions of the trinity. They are very distinct in their differences but are completely *one.*

Then came the temptation and fall of 'adam. Their eyes were opened, they realized they were naked, and God made them clothes. After the curses following the fall of man were pronounced, something astonishing happens. Genesis 3:20

says, *"And Adam called his wife's name Eve..."* I can imagine all the air being sucked out of the room. The animals that were walking or flying around must have gone completely silent. *A different name for Eve than for Adam?* I wonder what God Himself thought of Adam's freedom to name his wife something other than woman.

Eve was not named something separate from Adam before the fall. After the fall, their unity was broken, and they became two separate beings. So separate, in fact, that Adam felt compelled to give her a *completely different name from his own.*

Can you imagine the disastrous implications of how the woman must have felt? She had *never had a separate name* before.

Thank God, He didn't leave us there: two distinctly different people trying hopelessly to be one again. Jesus came to restore everything that Adam lost! Jesus is known as the "second Adam," because He came to the earth to restore exactly what Adam could not fulfill. The Apostle Paul wrote this truth to the Corinthian church:

*"And so, it is written, "The first man Adam became a living being." The last Adam became a life-giving spirit. However, the spiritual is not first, but the natural, and afterward the spiritual. The first man was of the earth, made of dust; the second Man is the Lord from heaven. As was the man of dust, so also are those who are made of dust; and as is the heavenly Man, so also are those who are heavenly. And as we have borne the image of the man of dust, we shall also bear the image of the heavenly Man."*

## Unity

-1 Corinthians 15:45–49

We no longer bear the image of the man of dust, who failed in his temptation, but we bear the image of the heavenly Man, Jesus, who restored what Adam lost. This means that by faith, we can once again enter a true unity in marriage that Adam and Eve had before the fall: a place where they were known by one name: 'adam.

This is why the Apostle Paul could write the very same command that God gave Adam and Eve in the beginning, before they had different names, to the church at Ephesus. Ephesians 5:32 says, "For this reason a man will leave his father and mother and be united to his wife, and the *two shall become one flesh*." Jesus made a way for the original command to be reinstated.

This revelation has done more for my marriage than the fifteen books on my bookshelf. When I see my husband as a part of me, it's hard to stay angry at him. It's hard to discount him or throw him under the bus, because I don't think that way about myself. When we truly understand that God wasn't exaggerating when He said 'the two shall be one flesh,' and we simply begin to rest in that union, we finally start to experience the reality.

Trust me, I'm not there yet. But I can honestly tell you that since this revelation hit my heart, I sense my heart has changed dramatically when I think of my husband or interact with him. I have hit a grace realm where I see that the vision that God has for us is to "be one."

| **State of Relationship** | **The Identity (Name)** | **The Perspective (Vision)** |
|---|---|---|
| **Original Unity**<br>(Gen 2) | **One Name:** Both were called *'Adam*. | **Bone of my Bone:**<br>Seeing the other as an extension of self. |
| **The Fall**<br>(Gen 3) | **Two Names:** Adam gives Eve a separate name. | **The "D" Word:** Separation, blame, and "us vs. them." |
| **TheLast Adam**<br>(Eph 5) | **One Body:** Reinstated into the Name of Jesus. | **Christ in You:** Seeing the other through the finished work of the Cross. |

Without vision, people perish. Marriages perish, families perish, and the impossible seems far out of reach. However, when we have God's vision instead of our own, that's when it's possible to enter the realm of the impossible. Wherever He calls us to, He equips us for, and grace is released in our lives to begin to operate and experience these truths.

Can you now see a vision for your marriage you couldn't before? Release faith for the grace that comes at this revelation and stand and agree in prayer over these words. May all our marriages reflect the oneness that God has called us to!

## The "One Another's"

Marriage is an important topic to touch on, but I know many of you are not married, or perhaps were and are now divorced. Scripture has a lot to say about how we relate to one another in general. There are so many other relationships in humanity to explore. How do we go about handling them?

I once went through a course on pioneering disciple making movements. In the course, one of the lessons we took was one on the "one another's." It hit my heart so hard, I knew I had to include it in this book.

In Matthew 22:27-39 Jesus said that the greatest commandment that we have is to love God, and to love our neighbor. The *greatest commandment* we have is a "one another" command! Just as much as God cares if we love Him, in the same breath, He cares how we care for others.

In the course I took, we were invited to search out every time a “one another” was used in the New Testament. The non-exhaustive list we were given had many scriptures, all with the words “one another” in them. After doing the lesson, I went back and looked for more. I found 59 “one another’s.” I have listed all of them in the following pages.

I want to invite you to do something unusual here. Don't skim this next section. Don't treat it as a reference list to glance at. Read it the way you'd read a letter written to you personally — slowly, letting each one land. I'll warn you: some of these will comfort you. Some will convict you. Some will feel impossible. *That's the point.* These aren't suggestions. They're the architecture of what oneness actually looks like between people.

- **John 13:34-35:** "**Love one another**; just as I have loved you, you also are to **love one another**."
- **John 15:12:** "This is my commandment, that you **love one another** as I have loved you."
- **John 15:17:** "These things I command you, so that you will **love one another**."
- **Acts 15:39:** "And there arose a sharp disagreement, so that they separated from **one another**."
- **Romans 12:10:** "**Love one another** with brotherly affection. **Outdo one another** in showing honor."

- **Romans 12:16: "Live in harmony with one another.**"
- **Romans 13:8:** "Owe no **one anything**, except to **love one another**..."
- **Romans 14:13:** "Therefore let us not **pass judgment on one another** any longer..."
- **Romans 14:19:** "So then let us pursue what makes for peace and for **mutual upbuilding**."
- **Romans 15:5:** "...grant you to **live in harmony with one another**..."
- **Romans 15:7:** "Therefore **welcome one another** as Christ has welcomed you..."
- **Romans 15:14:** "...competent to **instruct one another**."
- **Romans 16:16: "Greet one another** with a holy kiss."
- **1 Corinthians 7:5:** "Do not **deprive one another**..."
- **1 Corinthians 11:33:** "...wait for **one another**."
- **1 Corinthians 12:25:** "...that the members may **have the same care for one another**."
- **1 Corinthians 16:20: "Greet one another** with a holy kiss."

- **2 Corinthians 13:12:** "**Greet one another** with a holy kiss."
- **Galatians 5:13:** "...but through love **serve one another**."
- **Galatians 5:15:** "But if you **bite and devour one another**, watch out that you are not consumed by **one another**."
- **Galatians 6:2:** "**Bear one another's burdens**, and so fulfill the law of Christ."
- **Ephesians 4:2:** "...with all humility and gentleness, with patience, **bearing with one another** in love."
- **Ephesians 4:25:** "...speaking the truth to **one another**..."
- **Ephesians 4:32:** "**Be kind to one another, tenderhearted, forgiving one another**..."
- **Ephesians 5:19:** "**Addressing one another** in psalms and hymns and spiritual songs..."
- **Ephesians 5:21:** "**Submitting to one another** out of reverence for Christ."
- **Philippians 2:3:** "...but in humility **count others more significant than yourselves**." (Implied 'one another' in the action).
- **Colossians 3:9:** "Do not **lie to one another**..."

- **Colossians 3:13: "Bearing with one another** and, if one has a complaint against **another**, **forgiving each other**..."
- **Colossians 3:16:** "...**teaching and admonishing one another**..."
- **1 Thessalonians 4:9:** "...for you yourselves have been taught by God to **love one another**."
- **1 Thessalonians 4:18:** "Therefore **encourage one another** with these words."
- **1 Thessalonians 5:11:** "Therefore **encourage one another** and **build one another up**..."
- **1 Thessalonians 5:13: "Live in peace with one another**."
- **1 Thessalonians 5:15:** "...but always **seek to do good to one another** and to everyone."
- **2 Thessalonians 1:3:** "...because your love for **one another** is increasing."
- **Hebrews 3:13:** "...but **exhort one another** every day..."
- **Hebrews 10:24:** "...and let us **consider how to stir up one another** to love and good works."
- **Hebrews 10:25:** "...but **encouraging one another**..."

- **James 4:11:** "Do not **speak evil against one another**..."
- **James 5:9:** "Do not **grumble against one another**..."
- **James 5:16:** "Therefore, **confess your sins to one another** and **pray for one another**..."
- **1 Peter 1:22:** "...fervently **love one another** from the heart."
- **1 Peter 4:8:** "Above all, keep loving **one another** earnestly..."
- **1 Peter 4:9:** "**Show hospitality to one another** without grumbling."
- **1 Peter 4:10:** "...**serve one another**, as good stewards of God's varied grace..."
- **1 Peter 5:5:** "Clothe yourselves, all of you, with humility toward **one another**..."
- **1 Peter 5:14:** "**Greet one another** with a kiss of love."
- **1 John 1:7:** "...and we have fellowship with **one another**..."
- **1 John 3:11:** "...that we should **love one another**."
- **1 John 3:23:** "...and believe in his name and **love one another**..."

- **1 John 4:7:** "...because love is from God... let us **love one another**."
- **1 John 4:11:** "...we also ought to **love one another**."
- **1 John 4:12:** "If we **love one another**, God abides in us..."
- **2 John 1:5:** "...that we **love one another**."

Fifty-nine commands. And almost every one of them requires another person to practice on. You cannot "bear one another's burdens" alone. You cannot "forgive one another" in isolation. You cannot "outdo one another in showing honor" without someone in front of you to honor. Oneness is not an interior spiritual achievement — it is a contact sport. It happens in the friction and the beauty of real, daily, chosen relationship.

Before you rush on to keep reading, really stop and soak all those scriptures in and think about the implications of them. The Old Testament had 632 commandments, but the New Covenant just had two: Love God, and love others. In Matthew 22:37-40, Jesus said, "*You shall love the Lord your God with all your heart, with all your soul, and with all your mind. This is the first and great commandment. And the second is like it: "You shall love your neighbor as yourself."*

God has *so much to say* about how we treat one another. These commands are not transactional, but highly relational.

Transactional are things we do to receive or give something. In other words, “If I give money, you will do a service for me.” Or, “If I run an errand for you, you owe me.”

Relational commands are how we relate to one another in our daily lives. For example, when the Bible tells us to **'love one another,'** it isn’t a task to be checked off a list to stay in God's good graces. It’s an invitation to let the sap of the Vine flow through our branch into another.

The only way to walk out the “one anothers” is to... well, do life with *one another* intentionally and purposefully. You can't 'transactionally' fruit; you can only 'relationally' grow.

In the Kingdom, we don't 'network,' we 'neighbor.' Transactions happen at a counter, but transformation happens at the table.

How do we go about following these commands? 1 John 4:19 says, “We love Him because He first loved us." If you are not loving others well, it’s because you really don’t know how much God loves you. Our capacity to love—both God and one another—is not initiated by us, but is a *response* to the prior, unconditional, and self-giving love that God shows toward us.

We love others as we love ourselves. If there is a love deficit problem, it’s not on God’s end.

Take a moment to think about the friends and family you have in your life. Are you "one anothering" well? If not, how can you begin to receive the love of God in a new way so that you are able to love others well?

## Unity Through God's Eyes

I was invited to lunch with a friend. I said "yes" to the invitation not out of desire, but out of obligation. This friend and I have a past of mutual respect, but conflict and some turmoil. She and I disagreed doctrinally on some large biblical principles, and I was hesitant and guarded to speak to her about anything the Lord was showing me. In the past, if I tried to speak about a treasure of revelation the Lord had given me, I would leave feeling dishonored and unheard. Eventually, I stopped sharing the deeper things of my heart with this friend.

We'd both hurt each other deeply, so the relationship was fragile, and the relationship was divided.

The morning that we were going to meet, the Lord was beginning to teach me about the heart throne. He was showing me how the eyes of my understanding were in my heart, and He asked me that morning, "are you ready to see how I see, Kari?"

Upon arriving at the restaurant, I sat down, and my friend and I began to talk. She was expressing her heart about a situation within their church and asking for prayer. I gave her a light-hearted response with no real weight to it, nervous that I would somehow encourage what I perceived to be her wrong doctrine with my support. Even though the woman was asking humbly for prayer, I judged her in my heart as being mostly wrong, and I being mostly right.

Before we left, she said, "Kari, would you pray with me about this situation?"

Of course I would.

As I closed my eyes, I opened my mouth to begin to speak. What happened next was shocking and had never happened to me before. Instead of praying from my brain, as soon as I closed my eyes, I began to pray from my heart throne. My "spiritual eyes" took over, and my heart began to melt in the love and mercy of God. Tears unexpectedly ran down my face as I felt a river of the love of God begin to flow through me. Suddenly, the woman who stood before me was no longer doctrinally wrong, but I saw her heart as being perfect, precious and holy.

As I prayed, I began to prophecy destiny and life over this woman. I quoted scriptures I didn't even know that I knew. All the while, my brain was screaming at me, "Don't encourage her like this! She'll think that her doctrine is right, and she will infect other Christians with that bad theology!"

My brain didn't win the fight, and the words just kept coming. Before long, we were both a pile of tears, swimming in the manifested presence of God.

The division was gone, the air was clear, and for the first time in my life, I saw her as God sees her: not for her past mistakes. Not for her bad theology. Not for how many times she got it wrong in my eyes, but for the potential of her destiny in God.

The law always wants to measure people up, and find them lacking, but love covers a multitude of sins.

As I got in my car to drive home, the voice of the Lord boomed inside me: "Kari, now can you see how I see?" I was completely overwhelmed with God's love for this sister in Christ. I wanted nothing more than to encourage her, support her, and champion her. Until this point in my life, I did not know by experience that God's love had such tremendous power.

---

*What I was learning at home privately with the Lord manifested in the most powerful way in public.*

---

What I was learning at home privately with the Lord manifested in the most powerful way in public. What He whispered in my ear was shouted from the rooftop. No textbook can teach you what I learned in those five minutes of prayer, but I had to gone and learned what He meant.... "I desire *mercy*."

Paul says, *"For I determined to know nothing among you but Christ and Him crucified"* (1 Cor 2:2). I want to point your attention to the portion of the verse that says, "among you." I had always thought this verse meant that Paul determined to know nothing within himself but Christ and Him crucified, but that's not what that verse says in the original Greek. Paul is saying, "For I am determined to know (eido- to see, to perceive) nothing among you (en- a fixed position of rest) except Jesus Christ and Him crucified."

The Mirror Translation says it like this, "*My mind is fully made up about you. The only possible way in which I can truly know you is in the light of God's mystery, which is Christ in you. Jesus died mankind's death on the cross and thus brought final closure to any other basis of judgement"* (1 Cor 2:2, MT).

The only way I can truly have deep, lasting friendship is to see Christ crucified in the other person. Where we can honestly see another not for our faults, lack, mistakes- or even perceived wrong theology. But we simply see our brothers and sisters through Christ and Him crucified *in them*. Paul was saying from this point on, he was determined not to see anyone from a purely human standpoint. This is where mercy will triumph over judgement, and our opinions take a back seat to truth.

I could go on to the next attribute, but here is where we will pause. The rest of God's glory is described as gracious, longsuffering, abounding in goodness and truth (Ex. 34:6-7) ... each one of these adjectives is an encounter waiting to happen- an encounter that God wants *for you*.

## Unity

*Glory was always meant to be an experience.*

Paul the Apostle had such wisdom when he penned, "... "But God, who is *rich in mercy*, out of the *great love* with which he loved us, even when we were dead through our trespasses, made us alive together *with Christ*..."

In Christ, these encounters in the glory await you!

Seeing others through the perspective of Christ's sacrifice helps us embrace the unity and connection God wants for us. By choosing mercy over judgment, we can build deeper, more meaningful relationships that truly reflect God's love. May we all experience the glory of God in its fullest, encounter to encounter!

# CHAPTER FIFTEEN

## Glorious Mercy

My friend Andrew once invited our family to an impressive pizza place called DeSano's. This is not just any pizza place, but a fancy one where they make pizza with ingredients and ovens shipped from Italy. Their ovens are high-quality wood-burning ovens, and when you step inside the restaurant you see bags of flour stacked all over. Andrew assured me that this pizza would change my life. After taking my first bite of the pizza, I had to agree. It was so good; I teared up a little bit. Andrew laughed, and I, trying to justify my tears, said, "It's glorious."

Now, that pizza was incredible. Having personally tasted what Andrew told us about, I could agree it was by far the best pizza I'd ever had. But glorious? Sometimes I think we used words so far out of context and meaning that they begin to lose their meaning. What *is* glory? How does God use the word?

It's a term that many people have used and often used in scripture. The word glory in the Old Testament in Hebrew is the word *kavod*, which means weight or heaviness. It carries with it the idea of honor, importance, splendor and awe. The Greek word for glory is *doxa*, and it carries a connotation of radiance, splendor, and divinity. Sometimes it's best to investigate the definition so you can see if you're using the word appropriately- and yeah, pizza doesn't really fit the definition.

Although I appreciate dictionary definitions and concordance explanations, the word glory is more than a definition. Like the pizza- I could read the menu, but without tasting the description, it wasn't real to me. Glory is something talked about but rarely touched. Glory is something that was designed to be *experienced.*

In Jesus' high priestly prayer out of John 17, He didn't just pray that we would be one. He kept praying, and the next words out of His lips were *glory*.

Glory was given to Jesus by the Father, and that glory is what created the oneness that the Godhead shares. Jesus prayed, "*And the glory which You gave Me I have given them, that they may be one just as We are one: I in them, and You in Me...*" (John 17:22).

The same glory that The Father gave the Son has been *given to us*.

Why was glory given to us? So that we may be one, just as God is one, by being "in." As we are each "in Christ," we are also each "in" one another. The words "in Christ" appear approximately eighty-seven times in the New Testament, emphasizing the spiritual union we now possess and share with fellow believers.

The glory of God and oneness are both deeply connected.

The glory of God was on full display at Mt. Siani in Exodus 24:16, when the glory of the Lord settled on the mountain. For six days, the cloud covered the mountain. On the seventh day, the Lord called Moses from within the cloud. Moses waited for six days to hear the voice of the Lord and was rewarded with an astounding offer: God invited Moses into His glory. Can you even fathom how magnificent and fantastic this invitation was?

God invited Moses into His glory.

Once on the mountain, the Lord spoke to Moses face to face, as a man speaks to his friend (Ex 33:11). While on the mountain, Moses prayed, and we could see an inside view of his heart. Moses said, "*Now therefore I pray, if I have found grace in Your sight, show me now Your way, that I may know You and that I may find grace in Your sight. And consider that this nation is Your people." And He said, "My Presence will go with you, and will give you rest." Then he said to Him, "If your presence does not go with us, do not bring us up from here. For how then will it be known that Your people and I have found grace in Your sight, except You go with us?"*

So, the LORD said to Moses, "I will so also do this thing that you have spoken; for you have found grace in my sight, and I know you by name." (Ex.33:13-18).

God tried to give Moses an out: to leave and be with the people, but Moses was not willing to continue without the presence of God. Moses' desire was to remain in the presence of God, and to *know* Him, as God knew him: *by name.* To know God by His name, Moses knew that he had to ask one more question. This one question is about to unleash a side of God the Old Testament fathers did not know.

Moses said, "*Please, show me Your glory.*" (Ex 33:18).

I wonder what Moses was experiencing on Mt. Sinai as he prayed these words. Were his hands over his face, kneeling on the ground? Was he trembling, in awe of the cloud of God's majestic splendor? Was the wind of the Holy Spirit whipping around him? Was the mountain covered with fire and thunder and lightning? Was the mountain flooded with unapproachable light?

We don't have descriptions of what he saw, but we do know what he heard. God's response to Moses' glory plea was this:

*"... I will make all My goodness pass before you, and I will proclaim the name of the LORD before you. I will be gracious to whom I will be gracious, and I will have compassion on whom I will have compassion"*

Moses asked to be shown glory, and God's response was to *tell him about His name.* Here, God hides a secret for us to notice: *His glory is linked to His name.* God declared that his name was good, gracious, and compassionate. But that wasn't the full answer to Moses' question. Moses had to return the next morning and present himself on top of the mountain to the Lord. It wasn't enough just to hear God talk about His name and glory- but He wanted Moses to *experience His glory.*

Before Moses could return to encounter God's glory, God gave Moses some instructions. He told him that he could not see His face, and that he must stand on a rock. While God's glory passed him by, God would put Moses in the cleft of the rock and cover him (Ex.33:20-23). Remember how Jesus was the bread that fell from heaven? This is another prophetic shadow of Jesus, now described as the rock, hiding us. Jesus is always revealed by the glory.

Why hide Moses in a rock before the glory of God passed by? Because it is dangerous to try to see the Father without first being surrounded by the Son. If you only read the Old Testament, you'll see that God is often described as angry, judgmental and "fire and brimstone." If that's what God is really like, it will cause you to pull back out of fear, which is why the nation of Israel refused to climb the mountain with Moses.

Exodus 19:16-19 describes what the people saw that day: a thick cloud, loud trumpets, and lots of trembling people. Mt. Siani was covered with smoke, and the smoke billowed up from it like smoke from a furnace, and the whole mountain trembled violently. The sound of the trumpet was growing louder and louder. They were terrified! Fear will always cause you to pull back from love.

---

*Fear will always cause you to pull back from love.*

---

They weren't covered in the cleft of the rock.

It is only through the Son of God- Jesus- that we can see what Abba Father is like. Jesus said, *"If you've seen Me, you've seen the Father."* (John 14:9). If you try to look at the Father without seeing Jesus, you will see Him wrongly. Jesus is exactly what the Father has to say about Himself.

God warned Moses that he could not see His face because no man could see Him and live. (Ex. 33:20) Again, another beautiful prophetic shadow of us dying and being raised in Christ. This is why Col. 3:3 says, *"For you died, and your life is now hidden with Christ in God."* Once you see the face of God, that selfish nature of yours is forever dead, replaced with a perfectly righteous, new man *in* Christ!

I don't want you to miss the pattern that God is showing us in the Old Testament. Before God allowed Moses to experience glory, *He had to be surrounded by the Rock.* Before we can truly experience the glory of God, we must have a personal revelation that we have died, been buried, and then raised with Christ, and now share newness of life with Him!

- Gal 2:20: *"I have been crucified with Christ and I no longer live, but Christ lives in me."*
- Romans 6:4-5: "*We were therefore buried with him through baptism into death in order that, just as Christ was raised from the dead through the glory of the Father, we too may live a new life. For if we have been united with him in a death like his, we will certainly also be united with him in a resurrection like his.*"

With Moses safely hidden in the cleft of the rock, God could now reveal His glory:

"*The LORD descended in a cloud and stood with him there and proclaimed the name of the LORD. And the LORD passed before him and proclaimed, "The LORD, the LORD God, merciful and gracious, longsuffering, and abounding in goodness and truth, keeping mercy for thousands, forgiving iniquity and transgression and sin..."* (Ex. 34:5-6).

The first words that Moses heard when the glory passed by, hidden in Christ, was that *God is merciful.*

I once heard a man speak about mercy that deeply impacted me. The man had been instructing his children about the power of God's mercy for a few weeks and was asking God to teach him more about mercy. At the time, he had four young boys. One of his boys was around eight years old, and he was roughhousing inside the house when a family heirloom broke. He had been repeatedly warned by his father not to throw the football around, but he persisted, and now there was a shattered, precious family vase that was irreparable.

Angry, my teacher reached out to grab his son, yanked him back to the side room, and threw him over his legs for a spanking.

The eight-year-old squirmed and wriggled and tried to get away, but the dad firmly held him down, to no avail. The spanking was coming because *the punishment was deserved.* Unrelenting, my pastor lifted his hand with the belt, ready for the blow, holding down his squirming boy with the other.

Suddenly, the cries to stop turned into one loud, piercing plea. "MERCY!!!" The young boy screamed out of absolute desperation. "MERCY!! DADDY, GIVE ME MERCY!!"

The father stopped dead in his tracks, dropped the belt, and pulled his young son into his arms and held him, now sobbing and crying. His cry to have God teach him about mercy was answered that day.

The amazing thing about mercy is what the word itself means. It is translated in many ways through scripture. Sometimes, it's translated favor, goodness, or loving-kindness. It's also translated many times as kindness. But the root of the word itself is all those translations- and more. The word in Hebrew is "chaced," and it means to "bow the neck down as a courtesy to an equal."

*Can you picture God doing this for us?*

God Almighty, Sovereign, Kingly, all-powerful and all-knowledgeable, bows His neck down to us- and considers us His equal. This is incredibly significant because in biblical times of war, the conquering king would put their foot on the neck of the defeated king. Often, it would then result in the neck being cut off- but God does the opposite.

With His conquering mercy, he bends His neck down to our lowest places of defeat, raises us up and calls us His equal.

Hearing the words "merciful" is not enough. Merciful is an adjective meaning it's something that God *does.* Mercy cannot stand alone as a noun, but it is an action- a "doing." In the glory, we understand God being merciful to us as an *experience*, not just a theology.

One day, I was praying and asked God to *show me* His mercy. Although I knew about mercy theologically, and I knew by faith that God had been merciful to me, I wanted to have personal *experience* with His mercy.

The moment the prayer left my lips; I found myself in a memory of when I was in the psych ward over twenty years ago. I was on suicide watch, so everything I could have used to hurt myself was taken away from me. There were no strings in my hoodie, no shoelaces, or mirrors of any kind. In my memory, I remember walking into the bathroom to brush my teeth wearing a red hoodie I used to love.

Because they didn't allow mirrors, where a mirror would normally be in this bathroom was this plastic film in which I could barely see myself. At that moment in my vision, I saw Jesus standing right next to me, reaching to hold my hand.

In one of my deepest moments of emotional and psychological pain, where I wanted to destroy the temple of God in myself, He was there. Tears ran down my face like a river as I was awakened to the reality of His presence. When I least deserved it, when I least expected it, and when I most needed it, *He was there.*

---

*When I least deserved it, when I least expected it, and when I most needed it, He was there.*

---

Jesus didn't meet me in my darkest place with a wagging finger, telling me to shape up. He didn't look down His nose at me and say, "I can't believe you tried to ruin what I built. How could you?" No, His eyes in the mirror were full of so much love and acceptance that I was undone. Mercy, for me, was no longer theology, but an experience. *His kindness overwhelmed me.*

If mercy is just theology, you'll be hard hearted and hateful. Knowledge puffs you up, but love edifies (1 Cor. 8:1). There is something about an experiential process that moves the heart in a way nothing else does. Why else are we not content to just see pictures of the Caribbean, but we must travel there? Why else can we not just see photos and videos of the Grand Canyon, but we must travel there? Because *nothing* compares to first-hand experience. God hard-wired humanity for the experiential realm.

---

*God hard-wired humanity for the experiential realm.*

---

You cannot give someone what you have not experienced. Head knowledge won't do. Textbooks can't survive here. Hearing about God's mercy from another but not tasting its sweet flavor on your lips doesn't cut it. You need to personally experience the King of Glory bending down in the dirt you were found, holding you by the neck and lifting you out. Lifting you out of the mess you made, the consequences you deserved, and the turmoil you chose.

Once you see His eyes, looking at you with nothing but compassion and deep love- while being encased in mirey mud of sin- you will never be the same. The King of Glory, the merciful one, then robes you with a priceless robe, puts shoes on your feet, gives you His ring of authority, and seats you at a banquet table of a victory you did not earn.

## Jaw- Dropping Mercy

If Jesus prayed that we would be one, and that oneness is found inside of His glory- and the first thing that glory can be described as is merciful, we need to explore mercy. To have any kind of relationship flourish, one must be well acquainted with mercy. Remember that when God first introduced Himself to Moses, the very first attribute He listed was, ".... I am merciful..." (Exodus 34:6).

All the finished work of Christ has been accomplished. If you are saved, you have participated in the life, death and resurrection of Jesus. You have been made a brand-new species in God, completely reborn into newness of life. Everything needed for this new life in Christ has been purchased and delivered to us. It's ours for the taking! Why then do so few people seem to walk out this newness of life?

One reason is because they do not understand the mercy of God.

One of the most polarizing and captivating things about Jesus was His message of mercy over judgement. When Jesus came, He did not confront the Roman government. He not did try to be elected governor or stage a hostile, military takeover. Jesus did not even try to sit in Moses' seat. (Matt 23:1-3). When He came, He openly confronted the Pharisees.

In Matthew 23, Jesus delivers a scathing rebuke to the Pharisees and teachers of the Law. He pronounces seven woes upon them for their hypocrisy and misleading teachings. They prioritized legal minutiae over justice, mercy, and faith. Outwardly, they appear righteous, but inwardly, they are corrupt. They block others from entering the Kingdom of Heaven, and they exploit the vulnerable and persecute God's prophets.

In Matthew 9:13, Jesus responds to the Pharisees who criticized Him for associating with tax collectors and sinners. They were focused on external religious rituals and sacrifices (the law), but Jesus emphasized something deeper and greater. Jesus says, "*Go and learn* what this means: 'I desire mercy, not sacrifice." Go and learn? That sounds very different from just grabbing another goat and bringing it the priest so that it would die to cover their sin. Bringing a sheep to kill is easing. Going and learning is very difficult, intentional, and a long process.

---

*Going and learning is very difficult,*
*intentional, and a long process.*

---

When Jesus said to "go and learn," He was quoting an Old Testament prophet, Hosea.

Hosea was a prophet who prophesied for 60 years. God called him and chose him to do something no other prophet had done. Can you imagine his excitement? I'll bet he was so enthusiastic- eager to hear the assignment. Who do I get to prophecy to, God? Do I get to call down fire from heaven, or maybe do miracles like Moses? Do I get to lead your people into victorious battle, or by my prayers help deliver an entire nation? Do I get to multiply a widow's oil, or raise someone from the dead?

God says, "Here's your assignment, Hosea. *Marry a harlot.*"

I'm not sure what his reaction was to hear his assignment, but we do know Hosea was willing and obedient to the voice of the Lord. He married a harlot named Gomer.

Hosea's marriage to Gomer, a woman described as unfaithful, is a powerful symbol of God's relationship with Israel (and subsequently, us). Just as Hosea remained faithful to Gomer despite her infidelity, God remained faithful to Israel despite their unfaithfulness. This marriage exemplified the depth of God's mercy and willingness to forgive.

Because of Hosea's unique prophetic situation, we get exclusive scriptures describing the mercy of God all the way back in the Old Testament. Hosea 6:6 says, "For I desire mercy, not sacrifice, and acknowledgment of God rather than burnt offerings."

Consider, for a moment, what the word "desire" means. The Greek word for desire is "thelo." It means: to determine; to choose; to prefer; to delight in desire; to intend; to love. This desire is not the kind of desire like "I desire pizza for dinner." This kind of desire is passionate, unending, delightful, and filled with intentional love!

How could Hosea know God as a God of mercy, when many other prophets presented Him as a God of wrath and retribution? I think because Hosea had days, months and years of intentionally meditating on mercy- because *he had to.* Hosea had gone through the pain of loving and choosing a harlot to be his bride. He was formed in love in a way that few have had the privilege: the one who should have been one with him gave herself to many other lovers.

What was produced in Hosea's heart is awe inspiring, jaw dropping, heart pounding *mercy.*

Jonah 2:8 says, "*When man regards idols, they forsake their own mercy.*" If Gomer ran away into the arms of another man, she ran away from Hosea. In running away from Hosea, she is also choosing to run away from the very thing she is craving: *merciful acceptance.*

Because she did not know who she was, and her value, she let men determine her value. That kept her running from man to man to find acceptance and love. She looked everywhere for the next man who would love her, and it destroyed her. We can never find acceptance in another human. If you do try to do that, you will begin to live your life according to how others desire you to live. When you do that, you're allowing someone else to be Lord of your life instead of God.

That, in turn, makes that person an idol. To Gomer, the men she was chasing became idols.

Gomer didn't just have a lust problem; she had a Lordship problem. She was trying to fill a 'Glory-sized' hole with 'human-sized' attention.

---

*We can never find acceptance in another human.*

---

In choosing other lovers as idols, Gomer *forsook her own mercy*- that was freely, readily available.

If mercy is the open door into oneness, we need to understand the high price we will pay if we allow idolatry to rule in our hearts. We cannot be a people of God like Gomer- who choose to run away from the mercy of God and seeking fulfillment, satisfaction and fulfillment of lusts from other sources. God alone must be the source, and we must accept His mercy.

Mercy is so powerful, in fact, that Paul specifically mentions mercy in the context of not losing heart. He said, "because we have received mercy, we do not lose heart." The Greek word for "lose heart" is the word "ekkakeo," and it means to be weak, to fail, or to be worthless. Mercy strengthens us to endure things that would otherwise cause us to draw back into condemnation and want to just give up.

I believe this is why mercy is so powerful as it relates to relational oneness. If you personally have not received the mercy of Christ, you cannot give it to another, thus resulting in division and losing heart. However, if you have received a revelation of the mercy of God, your heart will be strong, and able to withstand relational conflict in a healthy way.

The journey to understanding and experiencing God's mercy is a transformative one. It's about moving beyond mere theological knowledge to a deep, personal encounter with Him. Through stories like Hosea's and our own experiences of God's compassion, we start to grasp the overwhelming love that God extends to us, at our absolute weakest moments.

This mercy not only heals and restores but also empowers us to extend the same grace to others, creating unity and restoring peace in relationships. Experiencing God's mercy allows us to live in the fullness of His love, free from the chains of idolatry and condemnation, and grounded in the assurance of His unwavering acceptance.

# CHAPTER SIXTEEN

# Peace

There's nothing better than a soul perfectly at peace. Humanity aches for this place of perfection that few seem to attain. In fact, in 2022, 34.1 billion dollars were spent to find a peaceful state. It's not, however, just the price to try to find peace with counseling, products and programs, but also the cost of war. The Stockholm

International Peace Research Institute concluded that global military spending reached $2.4 trillion in 2023 — a 6.8 percent increase from 2022. Is your mind blown?

Peace seems elusive at times to us, but it's the place Jesus lived. He is, after all, the Prince of peace (Isaiah 9:6). I've heard hundreds of sermons over the years on Jesus' ability to sleep during a fierce storm on the Sea of Galilee. Everyone seems to really be able to relate to the disciples' panic but left confounded with Jesus sleeping. (Mark 4:35-44). Where did He get this deep peace?

The Holy Spirit is the one who ushers in this reality for us. Romans 8:6 states, "A mind focused on the flesh is doomed to death, but a mind focused on the Spirit will find full life and *complete peace.*"

*Complete peace?!* Surely, this is an exaggeration. Isn't that a fairy tale? Not according to scripture. The word "peace" in Greek is eirene, and it means "to join, one, quietness, rest-to set at one again." The word peace is often used to describe a dove-tailed joint when building furniture. The strongest furniture is made when the two ends of one side are intermittently fixed together. This fastening together of two parts is almost impossible to break without breaking the whole part- it's dove-tailed!

Peace is literally bringing two parts together to make them into one. *It is a unity that remains.*

All those billions of dollars spent on seeking peace and paying for war could have been resolved in the scriptures. Whose job is it to find this peace, and how do we go about obtaining it? 1 Thess 5:23 says, "Now may the God of peace Himself sanctify you completely..." God is the one who does all the work! He is the God of Peace brings wholeness and sanctification!

This peace was not just reserved so Jesus could nap and have a cool story. No, this storm breaking, chaos calming, lay you down in green pastures kind of peace that is life changing *for us*! In fact, the apostle Paul got to such a place in this depth of peace, that he was able to write, "... *none* of these things move me" (Acts 20:24).

How could Paul write that trials, tribulation and persecution did not move him? He had a revelation of God as his own peace! Ephesians 2:14 says, "For *He Himself* is our peace, who has made both one, and has broken down the middle wall of separation."

Christ has dissolved every definition of division *in Himself.* He did not just do this for our relationship with others, but *primarily* our relationship with God Himself.

Once we have experienced this fusion of union by the blood of Jesus, you can easily see how this would translate into our interaction with one another. *Just as* we were once far off and were brought near by the blood of Christ, so is every other relationship.

He made a way for oneness in denominations, marriages, friendships, political parties, in wars, in race, in religion and in every form of separation. This is for every single heart in every single home. This is for your marriage to your spouse, and my marriage with my husband. This is the peace that is accessible to me even when my spouse does not seek peace from God. I can be at peace, even if others choose not to seek God.

If you're struggling with division in any of its forms, look to Christ.

## God Doesn't Like Arguments

One morning, I got up to pray. Cozying up with my espresso and my pillow, I flipped open my Bible and began to read. Suddenly, out of nowhere, I heard Holy Spirit whisper, "Kari, I don't like arguments."

Stunned, I sat there motionless for a while. Then I said, "Lord, you don't like arguments?"

"No," He answered. "I don't like them at all."

It seems like such a simple statement, but it really threw me for a loop. As I sat and pondered what I typically do in an argument, it all made sense. I think my way is right. I raise my voice, stomp off, or even slam doors to get my point across. I would bring up the past and roll my eyes to signal my disagreement.

Often, arguments happen because of the need for control or power. People have a lack of emotional regulation, they're afraid of being vulnerable, afraid of being wrong, or just simply wanting the other person to acknowledge how they feel.

When I stopped to consider it, I realize that Jesus never did any of these things. Why had I been settling for all these years with trying to "win" a disagreement and shove my point in anyone's face? Why had I, for years, accepted arguments as part of married life, *completely missing that Holy Spirit hates it*?

I began to dive into the Word to see how Jesus handled potential disagreements. Jesus used questions for the Pharisees, parables for those with hard hearts, silence when faced with untrue accusations, and He spoke identity to those who were living lives contrary to their design. Take a look:

**Questions:**

When Jesus was with the Pharisees, He would disarm them by asking them questions. They were unable to answer his questions without compromising their position, so they had to retreat, saying, "We do not know." (Matt 21:23).

The Pharisees often used questions to trap Jesus- meant to force him into a position where he would either violate Jewish law or Roman law, thereby undermining his authority. Jesus used counter-questions to turn their traps back on them and expose the flawed logic or hypocrisy behind their challenge.

Jesus also used this method to move the discussion beyond a petty rule to the core principle of God's law. The Pharisees would try to make a fight out of religious doctrine, completely missing the point of the Scriptures.

Questions open doorways into people's hearts. Asking genuine questions shifts the focus from yourself to the other person, demonstrating that you value what they have to say. Questions provoke a response and encourage the other person to share.

In this way, many times you can disarm someone, learn new perspectives, or clarify to make sure you're hearing the other person correctly.

**Parables**:

Other times, He would use parables. Jesus often used stories that were designed to conceal the truth from people whose hearts were hardened while revealing it to those who were sincerely seeking truth.

After the religious leaders planned to kill him, Jesus told the Parable of the Tenants (Matthew 21:33–46), a story about a landowner sending servants and finally his son, who the tenants kill. The leaders immediately "perceived that he had told the parable against them."

In dealing with disagreements this way, Jesus showed that He was unwilling to compromise the truth for the sake of peace or popularity, even when it escalated the conflict. Parables allow people to pass judgment on the characters in the story rather than implicating themselves. When they realize the story is about themselves, they are then empowered to repent or to harden their hearts.

There is an incredible account of the power of a parable in the Old Testament: King David. When King David killed Uriah to gain his bride Bathsheba, David spent nine months being unrepentant. However, one day, God sends the Prophet Nathan to confront David for his sins of adultery and murder. Nathan does not accuse David directly at first; instead, he tells a story (a parable) to draw out David's own sense of justice.

Nathan tells David about two men in a city: one rich and one poor:

"*The rich man had a very large number of sheep and cattle, but the poor man had nothing except one little ewe lamb he had bought. He raised it, and it grew up with him and his children. It ate from his food, drank from his cup and even slept in his arms. It was like a daughter to him."* (2 Samuel 12:2–3)

When a traveler came to visit the rich man, the rich man did not want to take from his own abundant flock. Instead, "*he took the poor man's lamb and prepared it for the one who had come to him.*" (2 Samuel 12:4)

David burned with anger against the man and said to Nathan, *"As surely as the Lord lives, the man who did this must die! He must pay for that lamb four times over, because he did such a thing and had no pity."* (2 Samuel 12:5–6)

*"Then Nathan said to David, 'You are the man! This is what the Lord, the God of Israel, says: 'I anointed you king over Israel, and I delivered you from the hand of Saul... Why did you despise the word of the Lord by doing what is evil in his eyes? You struck down Uriah the Hittite with the sword and took his wife to be your own. You killed him with the sword of the Ammonites.'"* (2 Samuel 12:7–9).

King David, upon understanding the wrong he had done, quickly repented. The power of a parable is in its ability to define the truth without condemning a person.

**Choosing Silence:**

In situations where his opponents were clearly not seeking truth and had already made up their minds, Jesus chose silence. When brought before Pilate and the chief priests, who were making many accusations, the Gospel records that Jesus "made no reply, not even to a single charge, so that the governor was greatly amazed" (Matthew 27:12–14).

*In the face of unfair accusations, Holy Spirit can empower you to remain silent and not defend yourself.* Let God be your defender and your redeemer.

**Prioritize Reconciliation:**

While Jesus was tough on the Pharisees and their legalism, His response to individuals and his own disciples was always focused on grace, deep love, and reconciliation.

When his disciples were arguing about "who was the greatest" (how many arguments does this come from?!), Jesus did not simply yell at them. He took a child and put him in their midst. He used a child to teach them that each person has value, and to see that value, one must have humility (Mark 9:33-37).

What about the woman caught in adultery? When the woman's accusers (with impure motives) brought her to Him, He deflected their trap by writing in the sand and saying, "Let him who is without sin among you be the first to throw a stone at her" (John 8:7). After her accusers left, he didn't condemn her but instead urged her to "go and sin no more."

Jesus prioritized the person's internal condition and salvation over "winning" the argument. The point is never to win the argument. The point is to be able to see value in the other person the way Jesus was able to.

If you see any person as less valuable than someone else, you've started down a very dangerous way of thinking. That type of thinking, full grown, is what led to slavery of Africans, the Holocaust, and genocide many areas of the world. We must learn to value and love others for their creative value the way Abba loves and values us.

I want to invite you to use these four methods for dealing with a potential argument the next time you're tempted to respond quickly. Pause, and ask Holy Spirit which of these methods are needed in that moment. Is it a question? Does the person need affirmation? Are you to be silent, or maybe take some time to think of a parable to share your heart.

## The Storms Can Stop

I remember watching a snippet of a beauty pageant once. The judge asked a contestant what she desired most in life. She smiled and without missing a beat, she said, "World peace." Evidently, this answer became chiche as beauty pageant contestants borrowed this answer and it became a pop culture trend.

Not surprisingly, the answer hits the sweet spot of most people. While the word "peace" itself doesn't always top the major surveys on what people desire the most, they say things like they want stability in their relationships with family and friends. They also want mental health with the absence of turmoil or anxiety.

Bottom line? People overwhelmingly desire *peace.*

Peace is a fruit that can only be displayed by abiding in Holy Spirit. It's not something you can manufacture or try harder to do. In other words, you can't just wake up one day and decide that you're going to be a peaceful person. *Peace comes into you because you are in the Prince of Peace, and He is in you.*

So, why don't we experience it all the time? Perhaps it's because we aren't aware of the great potential of peace.

Anxiety is the great robber of what our birthright in Christ is. Philippians 4:6-7 says,

*"Be anxious for nothing, but in everything by prayer and supplication, with thanksgiving, let your requests be made*

*known to God; and the* ***peace of God, which surpasses all understanding, will guard your hearts and minds through Christ Jesus."***

Peace is a fruit with a unique quality: it can guard your heart and mind. I like to think about it like a little soldier-fruit who stands guard over my heart and over my mind. It is militant, never abandoning its post to give way to fears.

What does this look like when the fruit is fully grown?

Mark 4:35-41 describes a moment when the disciples were unglued and Jesus was unmoved. They were crossing the Sea of Galilee in a boat when a sudden, violent squall picked up around them. The waves were breaking over the boat, and it was quickly filling with water. The disciples, many of whom were experienced fishermen, were terrified and believed they were about to drown.

Meanwhile, Jesus was asleep in the stern of the boat, resting on a cushion. The disciples woke Him up in a panic, crying out, "Teacher, do You not care that we are perishing?"

Jesus then arose and issued a direct command to the raging elements. "Then He arose and rebuked the wind, and said to the sea, **'Peace, be still!'** And the wind ceased and there was a great calm (Mark 4:39)."

What does peace look like? It looks like Jesus being in a boat with a giant storm looming, and instead of the storm taking them down and destroying them, the peace in Him affected everything around Him.

The measure of peace in side Jesus was no match for the storm. What would have quickly taken out some fisherman was stopped in its tracks by a fruit of the Spirit: peace.

Are you in the midst of a storm? It's peace that stops storms, never anger. It's peace that stills violent wind and waves, not frustration. It's peace that obliterates the terror of something looming in front of you that looks like it may destroy you.

The storm didn't wake Jesus, but the fear of His friends did. He didn't have to 'reach' for peace; He just spoke from the abundance of what was already resting in Him. You have that same abundance.

The peace that Jesus has is the same peace you can have. That peace is inside of you. Jesus said in John 14:27 "Peace I leave with you, *My peace I give to you*; not as the world gives do I give to you. Let not your heart be troubled, neither let it be afraid."

The peace you're longing for? Jesus wants to give it to you. In fact, *He's already given it to you in seed form.* The potential for every kind of fruit rests in your heart right now, waiting for the sun of His face, the soil of His love, and the rain of His spirit to grow and mature in you.

You don't have to try to stir up peace. You can't force peace to appear. **You receive peace by abiding, and when you do, you can change the atmosphere around you *just as Jesus did.***

The journey toward peace and fruitfulness is not about waiting for external circumstances to change or for distant promises to be fulfilled. Instead, it is about realizing the authority and gifts God has already placed within each of us and partnering with His Spirit to transform our lives and the world around us. By embracing the seed form that come from abiding in Him, we become active participants in bringing heaven to earth—living out love, unity, and purpose each day, and shaping a future as bright as His promises.

# EPILOGUE

For many years, I believed Jesus would eventually return and make everything right. I felt disconnected from His return, frustrated by my circumstances, and unable to create any meaningful or lasting change myself.

As I have learned some of the things I've shared in this book, I see things completely different. I know understand that God has given me authority over my own life, my family, and community. If there is a problem, I've been put there to find a solution. I am a very active participant in creating the world that I live in.

Instead of waiting for some cosmic "maybe" someday, I now put my hand to the plow and tend the proverbial garden in myself and my own home. I realize that the truths that I grow in, I can help others grow in, and that truth will set us free to love *just as* God loves us.

Knowing that I have been empowered with the same Spirit that raised Christ from the dead fills me with daily hope when I used to live hope deferred. My heart used to be sick when I thought I had to wait for someone else to come in and rescue me and fix all my problems, but now I live with confident expectation of good every day.

As my relationship with Holy Spirit has grown and flourished over the years, I have found that God delights in having us as partners with Him- ruling and reigning in the earth. He loves it when we partner with Him to bring His kingdom to pass.

Jesus will come again, and when He does, we will all be one. However, what I know now is, God has equipped us with many tools and much knowledge to bring the kingdom of heaven down to Earth not in some sort of ethereal cosmic future, but here and now. We can live fruitful, healthy and prosperous lives today with our families and friends that display God's glory!

**Will you be one who chooses to be fruitful, unified, with Holy Spirit as your leader? If so, we have a bright future.**

# Other Books by Author

1. What I Wish I Would Have Known About Prayer
2. Psallo, Volume One
3. Psallo, Volume Two
4. Psallo, Volume Three
5. Psallo, Volume Four

www.ingramcontent.com/pod-product-compliance
Lightning Source LLC
LaVergne TN
LVHW100523110826
845146LV00002B/753

* 9 7 9 8 9 9 4 6 2 0 2 0 5 *